HOOVERING UP THE HOLY CARPET

~ AN ARTIST'S LIFE AND TRAVELS ~ VOLUME 1: THE ACCIDENTAL ARTIST

LINDA ALVIS

HOOVERING UP THE HOLY CARPET
An Artist's Life and Travels ~ Volume 1: The Accidental Artist

First published 2022 by Alvis Fine Art

Paperback ISBN 978-1-9160106-2-8
Ebook ISBN 978-1-9160106-3-5

British Library Cataloging in Publication Data

A CIP catalogue record for this book is available from the British Library.

To my brother John

CONTENTS

PREFACE

THIS BOOK COULD EASILY be retitled 'Travels with Mother' as she features so prominently, gamely agreeing to be included in most of my travels. However, 'Hoovering Up the Holy Carpet' is most appropriate as I may never have started my painting journey in pastels, that most tricky of mediums, without meeting with Peter Clay again and hearing his famous phrase.

I hope this story will inspire my readers to be brave in their artistic endeavours and possibly travel to wonderful places ... or just enjoy accompanying me on the journey.

***

Photographs relating to this book can be found on my website at www.alvisfineart.co.uk/books.

My paintings and further award-winning poems, inspired by these travels, can be found in the poetry book, *Dawn Rising*.

INTRODUCTION

A VOICE BOOMED ACROSS the gallery.

'Alvis!'

'What are you doing here? Get to my art classes. I would prefer a good Catholic but you'll do and we only use pastels as I have to hoover up the holy carpet. Monday afternoons in Clifton Cathedral.'

It was the summer of 1990 when Peter Clay, then retired Head of Art at Clifton College Preparatory School, called out to me in Bristol's Royal West of England Academy of Art. There was no escape from him, but what a fortunate meeting and one which turned out to be life changing.

I called in to tell Mum on the way home. Recently widowed, she had moved to be near me and my boys. Beaconsfield Road gave her a new lease on life.

'Mum, I'm going to Peter Clay's art classes.'

'Eeh, that's nice our Linda.' Mum's northern accent never really left her except when she was trying to be a bit 'posh'!

Unable to work due to a persistent virus but, with a lifetime's love of drawing, the prospect of joining Peter's class was irresistible. Up until then I had been concentrating on old-fashioned bobbin lace, and I so loved it, but this soon had to stop. Dusty pastels and spotless white thread do not combine well. Fingers have to be squeaky clean for lace making together with patience and time. It is a slow process.

Peter had typical schoolmaster's humour and what a character he was. At school he was famous for his frequently wielded large stick, 'the Persuader', as well as priceless humour and cheerfulness. He was adored by my three boys. One, especially, was no stranger to 'the Persuader', though luckily fairly fleet of foot.

Monday afternoon arrived and, for a short while, I joined a happy band of fellow artists all enjoying Peter's inspiring support. I really loved this class but as my energy began to flag it dawned on me that I could work longer and better on my own at home. On my increasingly irregular visits, Peter would say, 'Here she comes, Alvis Gloria rent-a-mouth, hardly ever turning up and when she does she takes the best place'.

We all loved being treated like naughty schoolboys. Dear Peter. He truly kick-started my career as an artist and the debt I owe him is enormous. It was a great loss to his family, his many students and the art community as a whole when he died suddenly in 2003. Years later, former classmates were still calling me 'Alvis'.

EARLY DAYS

C LUTCHING MY PENCILS AND waiting to cross the road outside the old Berkeley Restaurant in Queen's Road, I had just stepped off the bus from Kingswood with my grandmother, Nan Fry. In the late 1940s I was four years old, but so excited to draw in the Museum. There were stuffed animals, carts and, some years later, a complete gypsy caravan. It was a treasure trove.

I was living with my parents, Jack and Connie, above their cycle shop on Kingswood High Street and we were surrounded by relations. Nan and Grandpa Fry were further down the road in Honey Hill. Nan's sister, Flo Rocket and her daughter Gwen were a few doors along, with a younger sister, Ivy nearby. I never knew Auntie Flo's husband but I believe he died an early death. He was known as a 'quack doctor' who gathered herbs and plants for potions. Perhaps he had one potion too many. On their simple smallholding in Cock Road lived yet another sister, sweet Auntie Em and her husband Sid. He had been a gifted carpenter in his working days, but by then always seemed to be sitting by their large, open hearth, smiling broadly from under his flat cap. They were a gentle couple. Dark-haired Ivy, the youngest, and possibly the wild child, always hid her age and even collected her pension from a post office outside her area. Unlike her sisters she was keen to drive. However, whether apocryphal or not, the story is she took her driving test thirteen times, once even turning the car over. However, she eventually passed. I'm sure the sisters had brothers, but never any mention of them was made.

As a lad, my father often spent the weekends with Auntie Em and Uncle Sid, going on to school from there each Monday morning. Having no running water, Auntie Em would do all the washing in a large bowl and this was eventually emptied out over the garden. One Monday morning, eight-year-old Jack dashed to the outside lavatory in just his vest and underpants. As he ran back to the cottage, Auntie Em chose that very moment to throw out the washing water. Dad was drenched. Off to school he went with Auntie Em's large vest and bloomers pinned together under his uniform. Unfortunately, it was the day of the school doctor's visit. No one said anything, but Dad must have been thought a very poor boy.

Kind Auntie Em, always so welcoming, with bottles of pop and plenty of chocolate biscuits, had a very hard life. Her dream was to live in a small house with a front door that opened right onto Kingswood High Street. It never happened, and she died in that cold cottage with its dark well-trodden earth floors, but it had been a home full of loving warmth.

Kingswood born and bred, my father Jack was a shock and an enigma to his modest, strictly chapel family. With boundless mental and physical energy, he ruled the roost from the very start. There was much shaking of heads. Dad was only four years old when he heard about a new engine being delivered to Kingswood Fire Station. Immediately, he toddled off to see it and asked the firemen if he could have the old one. Then there was the swearing and the love of fires. This he attributed to time spent with the local blacksmith who had an enticing open fire, of course. It wasn't too surprising that he was an only child.

A clever boy, a great sportsman and loving all types of music, Dad eventually won a scholarship to Kingswood Grammar School, known then as 'The Cowsheds' because of its wooden buildings. As was commonplace in the 1930s, he left school early, aged only fourteen, to be apprenticed to a carpenter. He vividly remembered his 'initiation ceremony' when a certain part of his anatomy was rubber stamped!

Nan and Grandpa Fry sold bicycles from their shop on the High Street. Grandpa Herbert was one of five children who had all inherited either a house or business from their mother. She had been left a policeman's widow when the children were very young, but a tough entrepreneurial spirit enabled her to build a business from nothing other than wits, determination and just a few pounds. She started selling paraffin from her front room and soon progressed to a type of agency, acting as the 'middleman', operating a voucher scheme between a store in town and the people of Kingswood. Jack got on well with this Granny, though not so well with Grandma Wilmot, Nan's mother, who was by all accounts a formidable woman. She was said to have walked all the way from her Kingswood smallholding to Clifton 'to sell eggs to the rich people'. Jack would run away and hide or lock the front door when he saw her marching up Kingswood High Street.

Dad obviously had a concentration of entrepreneurial genes in his make-up, but these sadly bypassed his own mother Lucy, 'our Luce'. Poor Nan was a great worrier all her life, always seriously anxious, and called 'eccentric' by the family. Herbert, her long-suffering husband, was a mild sort of chap who sadly died before my brother was born. However, I remember him quite well and especially on one occasion. He seemed to be looking at me over Nan's shoulder, as Nan was saying 'She's alright'! I don't know what I'd done on that occasion, but I was often called 'harden'! A good Kingswood word. Grandpa had fought in Gallipoli in the First World War, contracting malaria which was to plague him for the rest of his life. My last memory is of him lying shrunken and yellow on a downstairs bed in their Honey Hill house. Poor fellow. In 1939 Dad was sixteen and too young to enlist, so he joined the local 'Dad's Army'. Then, on his eighteenth birthday, longing to travel and explore the world outside the semi-rural enclave of Kingswood, he enlisted in the RAF with his friend Reg Smart. In readiness for foreign postings, he was later sent to Heaton Park in Manchester where he met my mother, Connie Taylor.

Mum's family, the Taylors, were from the North East of England, proud Tynesiders living temporarily in Manchester. Her father, John Henry, was the son of a butcher in Newcastle upon Tyne and had his own dairy business. He eventually married my grandmother, Caroline May Duke, known to everyone as May, and had three daughters: Ella the eldest, my mother Constance, and then Joyce. Grandad was a gentleman in the true sense of the word, and a quiet 'tut tut' was enough to know that he was cross. He had previously been unhappily married and Ella was the daughter of that union. His wife was still alive in an asylum when he met May and they fell in love. The family later realised this was why they moved to Manchester where they were able to live as man and wife. They married secretly on the death of Ella's mother, which wasn't until 1967. Mum was in her 40s when she found this out, although it had been known within the wider family. She and Joyce took it well and laughed about it. They were grateful to have wonderful, loving parents and I think of it as a brave love story.

Dad arrived at Manchester's Piccadilly railway station having never left Bristol before and, rather lost, started looking for his billet. Asking the way, he was immediately surrounded by a crowd of people wanting to help. It was his first experience of the outgoing Northerners he came to love so much. He had never before met kindness like this. Even now, when I visit family on the North East coast and catch the bus into Newcastle, the air is filled with pleasant chatter, reminding me of happy birds in an aviary.

At first Dad was billeted with a kindly Jewish lady who longed for him to find 'a nice Jewish girl'! It was never to happen. Going to the 'flicks' in the 1940s was a twice-weekly event for the three sisters, but one week they decided on a Sunday concert at the local picture house, The Astoria. Performing that night was George

Elrick and his Band. Having taken their seats in the darkness, Ella noticed a lone Air Force boy in their row. She turned to Mum who was sitting nearest. 'Ee our Connie, give that poor boy a chocolate.' That was it. There would be no nice Jewish girl. They were married within six months, and I arrived just after their first wedding anniversary in 1944.

I'm sure Dad must have thought he was in heaven, taken in by this loving family who were such fun and so outward going. It was a rather large family at that time as my Grandma and Grandad took in many other family members during the war. With countless friends and relations always popping in after work or staying when on leave, Myrtle House in Kersal Road was a gloriously happy sanctuary.

It is hard to believe that it was only twenty-one years from the end of that wasteful and cruel Great War, which took such a toll on nearly every family in the land, to the start of the Second World War in 1939. Grandad Taylor fought in Italy, or 'Itlee' as he called it with his strong Geordie accent, and was wounded, carrying shrapnel in his shoulder for the rest of his life. His young brother Herbert was killed, as was Charlie, Grandma's eldest brother.

I have a photo of fresh-faced Charlie, his precious life and marriage plans all before him. With the photo I have his Victory Medal and the saddest document from the Record Office in York, dated 24th June 1921. Addressed to his mother, Mary, Mrs M A Duke of 44 Chatsworth Road, Newcastle on Tyne, it formally requests acknowledgement of the enclosed decoration on an attached form, part of which was to be detached and returned to the Record Office. The serrated edge is a poignant reminder of my Great Grandmother Mary's pain as she signed the form and tore it off to return as requested. She had the medal, but all she would have wanted was her darling bonny bairn. She had already lost her youngest son Robert, who had contracted typhus swimming with his brothers and friends in the River Tyne. Her husband, my great-grandfather, was rather a rogue I believe, straying away from home and leaving this dear hard-working lady to bring up ten children, five boys and five girls. She was of course adored by them and the wider family. Originally from Kent, Mary's ancestor was an Avenell, and believed to be a French Jewess, although little is known of her now.

REMEMBRANCE
Looking at the photograph,
his fresh and handsome features,
bright light of life as yet undimmed,
in sepia tones now captured.

That very night, his mother saw him.
That very night, he called her name
and then she knew
the price was paid,
her son for 'King and Country'.

"I am directed to transmit to you
the accompanying Victory Medal
with His Majesty's high appreciation
...of services now rendered."

The edge, serrated, there remains
to prove 'Receipt returned',
when all she wanted was her son,
her fresh faced bonny bairn.

Clouds of petals now descending,
drops of blood
and one is his.
Emblem of a life unlived,
yet loved
...and still remembered.

As a young girl in Newcastle, my grandmother May remembered taking her cousin Robbie's son Geoff for walks in his pram. How could she have guessed that this little boy would eventually become World Motorcycle Champion Geoff Duke, still regarded by some as a hero and remembered by motorcycle enthusiasts the world over. Poor Grandma was walking to school when a boy threw a pen. It struck her in the eye and she was blinded in it, and was in pain for many years. She eventually had the eye removed and had a false one instead. This she had to take out and wash regularly, and the eye socket of course. As a young girl I was fascinated by this eye and would sit by the sink as she washed her face. 'Take your eye out, Grandma,' I would ask. She never seemed to mind.

As with the First World War, the Second brought its own responsibilities and sadness. Mum started off her war as an auxiliary nurse, then later joined the Army Pay Corps. Never one to shirk duty, she had always been a diligent and good daughter, having helped her father in his dairy business from an early age. Grandma had her hands full with Ella, who could be difficult at times, and also the very sickly but spirited Joyce. Joyce cried continually from birth and although something was obviously wrong, no one knew what it was. There was a large hole in her heart, but this would not be found until she was in her thirties. Despite all, Joyce was a tough, feisty and beautiful woman. During the war, and never one to give in, she joined the Land Army, eventually even cutting down trees. Dad, in turn, became a wireless officer, and being a bright lad was sent off on various training courses. He was extremely surprised to find the class being sent abroad, mainly to the Middle East, when his posting was to somewhere called Babdown Farm. He had never heard of it. Later, sent for special training, he sailed on the *Queen Elizabeth* to Canada, disembarking in Halifax, Nova Scotia for New Brunswick. Incredibly he came across his boyhood friend from Kingswood, Reg Smart, who had just been commissioned and was about to be fitted for his officer's uniform. The next news Dad had of Reg was that he had been killed in a bombing raid over Berlin.

Against this backdrop of the war, and with my father absent in Canada, I was being lovingly raised and totally spoiled by my grandparents, Mum, her sisters, all those visiting relations, and Vic, our loyal collie. Without doubt, I was the centre of their world and safely cocooned from the tensions and pain of those times. Reading between the lines I was obviously a handful, but there were never any complaints, not from the immediate family anyway. Mrs Hallsworth, the next-door neighbour, had five children and she used to say, 'Ee Mrs Taylor. Your Linda is more trouble than all mine put together.' I was a frequent visitor, clattering down their garden path wearing my wooden clogs and making a beeline for their toy cupboard! Fussy over food and difficult to feed, I had been found sampling coal and the odd worm in the garden. Poor Mum. She had two babies to care for. My cousin Bill's mother Molly was in hospital. She had been evacuated from London and was of course staying at Myrtle House. Bill, a real bouncing baby, was six months older than me and loved his feed, downing his bottle in one go. 'Never came up for air,' said Mum. However, I was a trial and took about an hour to take just a few ounces.

When I started to walk I was thought to be flatfooted, and the doctor suggested I should wear clogs to improve the supposed defect. They had to be specially made with leather and wood as worn by the mill girls at that time. I often thought about those clogs, although I have no real memory of them.

Elderly uncle Fred Duke loved to look after me during his month-long summer visits, but I seem to have given him a hard time too. If he took me out in the perambulator, off would come my shoes despite his gentle pleadings and at home I would see if I could walk round the drawing room without touching the floor. As I trod the piano keys he could be heard saying in his quiet sing-song voice, 'Get down, dear!'. Sadly, I took no notice and he never thought of forcing me. A fading black and white photo shows me in my perambulator with Uncle Fred looking kindly and lovingly at me.

I have many memories of Myrtle House. Often there were other children around and the most vivid scene I have is of a boy with very short hair sitting on our loo. He was one of Auntie Ella's 'poor boys' who she used to take pity on and invite to tea. Dear Nell, who was to me the most loving aunt, had her difficulties. She never married, although she came close to it in the 1950s when a sailor, Bill, wanted to take her to New Zealand. She was emotionally vulnerable and couldn't bear the thought of leaving the family, and Grandma was worried she would be unhappy being so far away. Bill was refused, and off he went to New Zealand on his own. I often wonder how life would have been for her if she had taken the plunge. Sometime after this she had a nervous breakdown and never quite recovered. However, she loved me unconditionally. Often late for supper, Ella could be found fast asleep in my bedroom, book in hand, with me quite wide awake in the cot.

In 1946 the cosy bubble of my northern childhood burst. Dad was demobbed and although offered a commission in the RAF decided against it, wanting to go back home to Bristol to take over the family business. He was full of ideas for it, but also thought I was being ruined by the Taylors and had to be brought into line! Probably true, but how grateful I am for that loving start to my upbringing which helped so much to make me who I am today.

Grandma, Grandad, my aunts and the old dog Vic never quite got over our departure. One day Vic thought he saw Mum in the distance pushing me in the pram. Auntie Joyce watched him set off at such a terrific pace, ears up and tail in the air, only to slow down as he got closer, realising it wasn't us at all. Tail and ears drooping, he slowly walked back to her. Vic, a Border Collie, had been brought home by Grandad in his milk van, probably unwanted and given to him on his morning round by a customer. Grandma wasn't having any of it.

'I don't want a puppy around. There is enough to do' is what she probably said. Grandad and the girls kept very quiet and later saw Grandma give the puppy a drink. 'Poor thing,' she said. Vic was staying and, much loved, stay he did for 21 years.

Auntie Joyce was a brave woman who, in the 1950s, after having her two children Fraser and Avenell, and never having known what it was to feel well, had a major collapse. She then had an emergency and pioneering heart operation at the Freeman Hospital in Newcastle upon Tyne, where a Mr Mason, surgeon to General Eisenhower, performed the procedure – 12 hours in deep freeze! Just before her operation, this young woman would hold my arm to walk slowly and breathlessly down the slope from the Promenade onto the beach at Whitley Bay. I looked on in amazement as, quite soon after the operation, she actually ran up that same slope.

It must have been quite a culture shock for Mum when she first arrived in Bristol. Their Kingswood home was gloomily basic and snails crawled in the bath. She rarely complained and was lovingly welcomed by Dad's family. However, they were all so different to her own, and like most West Country people at that time, rather reserved.

Shopping was a fairly nerve-wracking experience. Mum remembered going to the wool shop for the very first time. Not a strand, needle or pattern could be seen, but on the counter was a large pattern book. Customers were not allowed to touch the book, the owner turning the pages herself. When the pattern and colour was chosen, wool appeared from under the counter, neatly wrapped in brown paper.

A slightly more unnerving experience was a visit to the haberdashery opposite. Here two spinster sisters preached to their customers from an open Bible on the counter, relevant passages underlined in red. This shop stocked a beautiful selection of items, but you had to really want something badly to brave going in. Customers already there were edging towards the door to make a hasty escape as the next customer entered. They in turn had to wait for another courageous soul to walk in before dashing to freedom.

Mum and Dad worked hard to develop the family cycle shop on the High Street and soon introduced a novelty: gramophone records. During the war Dad had taken an air force friend to a concert which included Debussy's 'Prélude à l'après-midi d'un faune'. Ever the romantic, Dad mused, 'Can't you just see the faun leaping through a dappled forest?' His friend retorted, 'Don't know what you're talking about, Jack!' Gramophone records were thought terribly sinful at that time, especially by his strict chapel-going relations in Kingswood. However, they sold out almost overnight. Popular hits, classical music and, of course, air force bands were a great success, as were the prams and toys which soon followed. In the austere post-war years luxury items were a breath of fresh air, although not always welcomed by some of the pious inhabitants of Kingswood.

I was not overly keen on musicals, but my very favourite song is still 'Some Enchanted Evening' from the original soundtrack of 'South Pacific'. I can see my four-year-old self leaning over the banister, listening to it being played down in the shop, and to this day it never fails to overwhelm me with a great wave of nostalgia. In 1949 my brother John arrived, a plump, sweet little boy who was always happy and good. Such a relief for Mother.

When I was about four years old we watched the massive Brabazon fly over Kingswood. It seemed to fill the sky over our backyard and, with its slow progress, appeared just to hang there. It was quite an event. As was around the time Dad drove us out to see a huge fire at Avonmouth Docks. His fascination with flames never left him and he was always happy when he had a good bonfire going. He only once let it get out of control. Back as a young married man, living in Myrtle Bank, he managed to set the fence on fire with a too ambitious mound of garden debris. Auntie Joyce was told to man the stirrup pump as Dad directed operations with the hose. Auntie Joyce, with her weak heart, would have been pumping for all she was worth whilst Dad, calmly hosing, put out the flames before the fence burnt down.

Mum continued to support Dad as he developed the business, working long hours in the shops yet still keeping the home running smoothly. I must have spent quite some time with Nan, as I clearly remember her house in Kingswood's Honey Hill with its blue forget-me-nots filling the garden. Each night, as I slowly sank into a huge feather bed, I watched patterns dancing on the wall from the streetlight as it shone through the net curtains. I would wander up to Auntie Gwen and Auntie Flo's house just a few doors up. They would regularly treat me to butter coated in sugar, saying, 'Ah, she's awright'. Spoilt again.

As the business continued to grow, Dad, who loved cars, was able to treat himself to a new model every couple of years. Only once did Mum complain when he turned up with a brand-new Triumph Roadster. Her foot came down very firmly. No way was she going to perch on the rear dickie seat with baby John. The Triumph went back to the showroom that very day. Dad eventually became the proud owner of a Bentley and later a Rolls Royce. These were short-lived experiences as Dad couldn't enjoy driving around in such obvious luxury when 'people are starving in Africa'. He eventually settled for Jaguars and Daimlers. Still pretty luxurious, but he felt more comfortable.

I was always terribly car sick, and what seemed like the permanent smell of new leather certainly didn't help. With Mum in the back with John, I sat in the front where Dad could keep his eye on me and make sure I followed the 'drill':

1. Select a bag;

2. Open it and be sick;

3. Tightly close bag by screwing the top;

4. Open window;

5. Throw bag out;

6. Points off if the bag breaks and splashes the car.

This was Dad's Law. How ghastly it sounds now, but nobody thought anything of it at the time. It would have been a paper bag!

The Taylors, distraught after we left for Bristol, soon returned to the Northumbrian Coast, settling near family in Whitley Bay. Kersal House in Roxburgh Terrace was then our holiday destination from 1946 for the next fifty years. It still has the most beautiful stained glass above the front door, made by the talented Jenkinson glaziers, our cousins. It wasn't unusual for us to visit Whitley Bay four times a year. Without motorways this was a marathon twelve-hour drive through all the major cities en route, with me being car sick all the way, regularly asking 'Are we nearly there?'. But oh, the joy of arriving. Turning the corner into Roxburgh Terrace, piling out of the car into that dear familiar house with its lovely smell of Grandad's tobacco, furniture polish and something delicious cooking in the back kitchen. Grandma, as always in her full-length apron, would probably be preparing our favourite scalloped potatoes with fish brought straight from North Shields Fish Quay that very morning. The local fishmonger often had cod cheeks. These were huge at the time but cheap and made tasty pies and fish stews. Grandma also cooked pancakes for us in her large black frying pan. We often wondered how she managed to make them so fluffy and tasty. Looking back I see that pan was rather full of fat, but the result was incredibly delicious.

As soon as possible John and I would be off to the nearby Spanish City Amusement Park, or to the beach. A favourite pastime was collecting winkles from the rock pools on St Mary's Island, but always with an eye on the tide which cut the Island off from the mainland twice daily. Careless winklers could be temporarily stranded and we had to make a dash for it on many occasions over the years. When the tide was out, bountiful clear rock pools demanded our constant attention. We spent hours examining their contents: red jelly-like sea urchins needed a prod; rocks had to be turned over so tiny shrimps and crabs scuttled out; seaweed bladders needed to be popped; and then there were the winkles – hundreds of them. We filled our buckets and took them home to Grandma. With never a complaint, she boiled them up and gave us each a pin so we could prise off the little caps and 'winkle' out the tasty, salty flesh. And then every afternoon Grandma would have a ten-minute nap on the sofa in the sitting room, her pinny flung over her head. Ten precious minutes to herself

From Manchester, Grandma's younger sister, Auntie Connie, often joined us with her husband Uncle Tom and cousin Diane. Diane, John and I soon got down to some serious drawing and painting. On one of these occasions Mum called Auntie Connie in to look. All three of us were completely absorbed by the job in hand. We hadn't noticed my little brother painting so earnestly that his brush was worn right down to the wooden stump. Not a bristle left and John still painting! And then there was Auntie Lily, the sweetest of women, sadly struck down with a severe stroke when only in her 30's. She lost the use of her right arm and leg and never spoke again other than to say 'By' and to hum tunelessly. Always smiling, Auntie Lily was a regular at Roxburgh Terrace after she was widowed, and on the numerous occasions I was confined to bed with some ailment or other she would sit with me, humming away and writing answers to my questions in the wardrobe mirror.

Pride of place in the sitting room was a wonderful old gramophone with thick steel needles. How I loved winding it up, placing the heavy head carefully onto the old 78 records. Always ready to give it a gentle thump when it stuck in a groove and then, furiously winding it up again as the music slowed down! So much happiness, with bracing sea air, the Venetian Ice Cream parlour, Spanish City amusements, wonderful beaches and countryside and all those relations. Oh, the tears when we left!

There was one wonderful occasion when Mum, Dad and John left Whitley Bay for Bristol without me. I was ill and not well enough to travel. I actually felt a bit homesick for about twenty minutes or so and was just a tiny bit tearful over my puffed wheat, but recovered soon enough to have a wonderfully happy term at nearby Park School. This was just a couple of streets away from Roxburgh Terrace and on my way home I would call in on one of Grandma's sisters. Auntie Bertha Jenkinson, mother of eight sons and three daughters, who lived right on the school route in Holly Avenue.

'Hello Hinny,' she would say as I opened the door. She adored children and would never recover from losing one of her youngest, Colin, in a motorcycle accident. I still remember Colin as a young man and seeing him at 41 Roxburgh Terrace just before his accident. He had poor sight and wore very thick glasses, and as a small boy insisted on wearing them at night because he 'wanted to see his dreams'.

Back in the 1930s, the beach evangelist, Uncle Pat, was a regular visitor to Whitley Bay. It was major beach entertainment, and he always drew huge crowds. Colin would be there and usually first up on the stage when singers were called for. Uncle Pat would ask the crowd to be very quiet as this little lad with a tiny voice was going to sing. The crowd hushed and Colin started up and out came this huge sound. His foghorn voice had everyone in stitches. It became an annual event.

Auntie Rene Newman was another of Grandma's sisters. I'm glad to say she had a well-established newspaper and sweet shop on Station Road. I often think of the thousands of visitors whose first port of call after getting off the train would be 'Newmans' before setting off for the beach with their new buckets and spades, fishing nets, sweets and ice cream.

I feel very sad now when walking though Station Road, Roxburgh Terrace and Holly Avenue. Such lovely memories when John and I were once one of the 'canny bairns'. Those dear people, so many of them, and now all gone.

SCHOOL DAYS AND BOATING

WANTING TO DO THEIR best, my parents had enrolled me into a small private school in Clifton, Amberley House in Apsley Road. I don't remember too much of it as, sadly, my time there was rather short. Every day, the school bus delivered me back to Kingswood High Street in a sorry state. I can see it all now, helped off by some kindly soul as, yet again, 'Linda has been travel sick'.

Dad must have said, 'There's no point in continuing this.' From then on my school days were interesting and varied, to say the very least.

We soon moved away from the shop to a proper semi-detached house in Wick. I went to the local school for a short while, and it was here on my battered wooden desk I actually used a slate to write on. By then my parents were slowly building up a thriving pram and toy business, eventually known as Fry's Baby Fayre, and as new shops were added we kept moving on.

The next stop was Fishponds Road. We lived above the shop again, part of a rank with Orchards Hardware next door. Recovering from chicken pox I happened to look out of my bedroom window to see Rex Orchard flying the Union Jack at half-mast from a flagpole just over their shop. King George VI had just died. My mother came up to see me a short while after, only to find my bedroom completely decorated with lengths of coloured wool draped from one light to another. I obviously thought, as the King had died, it was the thing to do.

Aged six and my next school was Chester Park School, a short walk away; also Sunday School in the nearby Methodist Church. I joined the choir and even now hearing 'All in the April Evening' brings a lump to my throat. The Methodist Church was very keen on 'The Pledge' and one Sunday these pledge forms were brought round to the Sunday School for us to sign away our rights to have a drink. After a brief moment's thought, and watching lots of children signing away their rights to a tipple, I decided I might enjoy the odd glass of sherry when I was grown up so declined the offer. I'm not sure how well that went down at the time, but nobody said anything.

Although we lived above the toy shop John and I didn't have lots of toys, but the ones we had were much loved. Representatives from toy firms would come to see Dad and leave samples for us. My Pedigree dolls were samples. I still have three of them. Elizabeth, the first, now shows signs of much attention and love with her hair cut short and wearing one of my own pink knitted baby dresses. Caroline was a step up, a walkie-talkie, still with her original dress and shoes. As lovely as she was, she was less cuddly and probably a bit cumbersome. The third was Julie, small and beautiful with long blonde hair and accompanying hairdressing kit. Her long tresses were often washed and set 'à la mode'! One day the rep arrived again and with two small dolls, one white and one black. How I loved them and often played on my own with them in the back street. One day I stood them close together on the pavement as I popped back into the shop yard. I was only gone for a few minutes, but when I came back the dolls were gone. It was a terrible shock and I stood there just looking at the empty space, but I said nothing to my busy parents and pushed them to the back of my mind. It was the only way I could deal with it. However, I remember them still to this day. I hope someone enjoyed them as much as I had done.

More shops around the West Country followed, until eventually there was a chain of twelve Fry's Baby Fayres. One occupied a central position opposite the Pump Rooms in Bath, where a young couple came in to order a white pram for their first baby. After no little difficulty it had eventually been acquired and stored in the basement awaiting the baby's arrival. The day came for the new parents to take delivery and the pram was brought up from the storage cellar and unwrapped, only to find it had turned a rather lovely shade of pink. Poor Dad; after all his effort, the minerals in the damp Bath atmosphere had affected the paintwork and the sale would surely be lost. I believe the air rapidly turned blue with expletives, but the music had to be faced and the couple informed. Miraculously, however, they were thrilled. The baby was a girl, and they were the proud owners of the only pink pram in the country.

Soon we were on the move again and to a semi-detached house in Cleeve Hill Extension, Downend. It was an interesting and close-knit community which, like a big family, had frequent weekend outings and cricket matches on Siston Common. One memorable day, when I must have been around nine years old, our next-door neighbours the Batesons included me in their family day trip by train to the Wye Valley. I have this incredibly beautiful memory, standing with them on the platform of a tiny station in a heavily wooded and perfumed green valley. The sun was shining and in the distance a man was singing, his voice echoing around the hillside. It was heavenly, and now seems like a dream.

Living in Cleeve Hill Extension I went to Downend Church School, my fifth by then, and one I loved. Mr Byfield was the kindly headmaster and Miss Brain my class teacher. Miss Brain was rather fond of face powder which she applied quite generously, and I was often sent down into the village to get her a powder compact from the chemist's. I must have done some work, but also became very involved in sport. I loved to run and was virtually unbeaten on sports days in the flat race, hurdles, relay and high jump.

Failing my eleven plus, which I suppose wasn't too surprising, my parents decided to try private education again and eventually, by the skin of my teeth, I won a place to Duncan House, a small private school on the Promenade in Clifton. Starting in the junior school aged eleven, I wasn't to leave until I was eighteen. My first stable and continuous schooling had begun and, for my parents, only three more house moves to go!

While we were living in Cleeve Hill Extension, Dad sold his chain of pram and toy shops to Lines Brothers of Tri-ang Toys. He was invited to work with them and joined their Board, but it was a short-lived occupation. He greatly admired the Chairman, old Walter Lines, who was, unfortunately, soon to retire. Dad just had to be his own boss, and so looked around for something else to do.

One day I came home from school to find the dining room floor and table covered with business brochures. We leafed through them, discussing which might be the most attractive and interesting. After considering many options, including a farm and garage, which I thought sounded rather fun as I could see myself manning the pumps after school, Dad decided on a newspaper shop in Brislington. Eventually other shops followed in Old Market and Henleaze, where he became the sub-Postmaster. Helping out in the shops on Saturdays, supposedly serving, I spent most of the time reading comics and joining Dad with our hands in the sweetie jars. These were the days of 'Girl', 'School Friend', and of course the iconic 'Dandy' and 'Beano'. How I loved those comics, spending most of my time leaning on the counter having a good read and feeling rather put out when a customer came in. It was around that time that I became a regular visitor to our dentist, Mr Sarafian in Staple Hill, where I had rather a lot of fillings!

Finances obviously improved and we soon moved on to a brand-new bungalow at the top of Blackhorse Lane, on the outskirts of Downend. Named 'Rothbury' after the Northumbrian village, it was one of only three houses in the lane. Our two neighbours were the Fuge family, orchid growers who had built our bungalow on their extensive land, and on the opposite side of the narrow lane, young Dr Fox and her family. Behind and in front of us, stretching all the way down the hill to the Trident off-licence on the main road to Chipping Sodbury, was countryside. Beautiful, wooded meadows were completely carpeted each spring with cowslips and bluebells, and these we gathered by the armful. Looking back it seems almost surreal, running up and down the steep fields with my brother and friends, laughing in the sunlight; and now especially poignant, with Blackhorse Lane fully developed and carpeted with houses instead of wildflowers.

We stayed in Blackhorse Lane for a few happy years, but then moved to a very fine house at the end of Lilymead Avenue in Knowle. As much as we loved this house, with its panoramic views over the city towards the famous Suspension Bridge, Dad couldn't stand urban living and all that traffic, so after about a year we moved again, this time to a detached house, 'Madron', in The Ripple on Tickenham Hill. Overlooking the village of Nailsea on the Clevedon Road, The Ripple was so-called because, as the people in the valley looked up, they could see the grass rippling in the breeze. As a boy Dad rode his bike from Kingswood to Clevedon and, looking up at The Ripple, decided he would live there one day. It was to be the final move, and my parents had twenty-five happy years there together.

The beautiful, third-of-an-acre garden seemed enormous. My bedroom looked out over the small but expanding town of Nailsea nestling below in the valley. In the distance was the unusually named St Quiricus and Julietta Church, with its boat mooring rings dating from the time the levels around Tickenham were under water. Leading off my bedroom was a store cupboard, and then a small door into a narrow roof space which I quickly made into a cosy den. It was here I decorated the walls with pictures and spent my time drawing and writing little stories. Apart from one over-romantic poem I have no idea what happened to them all, but in my early teenage years I spent many happy hours there scribbling away on my own.

Around the time of our move to 'Madron', Dad decided to get a boat. He had long wanted one and we soon became the proud owners of *Felicity Girl*, or *Facility Girl* as Grandad Taylor always called her. She was a single-engine 36-footer, built in 1951 by Theakes of Whitby, and based at the fledgling Berthon Boat Yard in Lymington, Hampshire.

Our boating years had a leaky start. The heavens opened on our very first weekend in Lymington and water dripped in, copiously. Luckily our bunks kept dry, but the rest was a sorry sight. 'I do commiserate with you,' assured Peter May, the boatyard owner, as he dropped by. The carpets were so wet I had to hang my fluffy pink slippers on the roof hatch handles in my cabin. Undefeated, we enjoyed years of happy boating around the Solent and Isle of Wight, and as confidence grew, embarked on further adventures across the Channel to Cherbourg and the Continent.

Our next boat seemed enormous and luxurious in comparison. It was the lovely *Avila*, a 43-footer built in 1961, with two Parsons Pike engines and definitely no leaks. She had two auxiliary sail masts which occasionally had to be lowered to pass under low bridges on our adventures along the Seine and in the Netherlands. On a visit to Honfleur, at the mouth of the Seine, we befriended a French family, the Le Baillifs, who were on a day trip from their home in Rouen. I can still hear Monsieur Baillif repeating 'Très jolie, très très jolie' as we invited them on board. The eldest daughter, Anne-Marie, became a lifelong and dear friend. Boats moored in French towns were always subject to great inspection, with families peering through the portholes and almost climbing on board to get a better look. I often wonder what made us ask *this* very family on board.

Of our many voyages, especially memorable was our trip along the Seine from picturesque Honfleur right into the heart of Paris, where we moored by the Pont Alexandre Trois. It was a romantic

and beautiful location. Another more ambitious holiday was a
month-long journey through Belgium and Holland into Germany,
where we planned to navigate the Dortmund–Ems Canal. Previously, at home, looking at the maps, we saw how many castles
there were marked along this route and looked forward to a
beautiful journey. It seemed so exciting... until we were actually
there. The 'schlosses' we thought were castles turned out to be
busy working sluices and locks with massive drops, some of 100
feet or more, all of which we had to navigate. It could have been
an arduous nightmare, but quite often we managed to tie up to
one of the huge German barges working the canal and descended
with them. It certainly made the descents less traumatic. When
we didn't have the good fortune of a kindly bargee alongside, we
had the anxiety of rapidly letting out the ropes that tethered us
to the land as we dropped down and down. Would the ropes be
long enough? Dad's ripe language bounced off the sluice walls as
he directed operations.

Once, while staying at Yarmouth on the Isle of Wight, Grandma's
youngest brother Uncle Ernie and his sweet, funny little wife Hilda
came for a short stay. Dad and I watched from *Avila* as Mum and
John rowed off to meet the ferry from Lymington. Eventually they
all arrived at the harbourside where our dinghy was tied up, and
we saw Uncle Ernie, well prepared for a cruise, wearing a navy
blue peaked cap and blazer.

Auntie Hilda was helped into the dinghy which was now swaying gently. She sat patiently holding onto the sides, waiting for the
others.

'Make sure you stand in the middle and not on the edge, Uncle,'
my Mother warned as Ernie, now a little portly, proceeded to step
in.

'Do you think I don't know how to get into a boat, our Connie?'
retorted Uncle as, at that very moment, he stepped onto the
edge and tipped the whole thing, including Auntie Hilda, into the
harbour.

Dad was furious. The Lines brothers were in port. Concerned less about the welfare of our visitors, his worry was who might have seen the embarrassing incident. A public capsizing in full view of the Yarmouth yachting fraternity was not the thing to do.

'I touched the bottom of the harbour,' said Uncle as he pegged his pound notes out to dry in the saloon. 'When I surfaced I thought, "where's my cap?", then "never mind the cap, where's my wife?" Hilda was safely rescued, of course, and laughed along with the rest of us.

Later Dad bought a new, 42-foot motor cruiser christened *Avila 2*. With a top speed of 18 knots she was 9 knots faster than *Avila*, but being modern in design had less character and, like the cars that were changed so often, within two years she was gone. Dad then acquired a new, very smart motor yacht which he named *Wessex Leader*. With this grand boat we enjoyed many years of glorious trips around the Solent and Isle of Wight, and still further afield to Cherbourg and the Channel Islands. Here we came to especially love Guernsey and the Beaucette Marina, which gave us a peaceful and very sheltered mooring. The entrance was very narrow, but with just enough width for boats our size to pass through. We were told the owner of the original water-filled quarry allowed the army to exercise there, and this included blowing a hole in the wall! The sea gushed in through the narrow opening, and the marina was born. It was quite a long walk from the marina to the main road, and a bus to St Peter Port, but on the garden walls of many of the houses we passed were large boxes of ripe tomatoes, peppers and cucumbers with the notice, 'Please Help Yourselves'. Happy days. Being fair-weather sailors, the shipping forecast became an important part of our daily routine. Dad was not one to risk uncomfortable conditions, and being a perfectionist with maintenance, he often quipped, 'You won't find a garage in the middle of the Channel'. I was First Mate, Mum was cook, and John helped Dad to make the boat gleam. To this day, John loves giving wood and metal a good buff-up.

My final school, Duncan House with its uniform of distinctive straw boaters was more of an establishment for young ladies rather than an educational hothouse. It was an imposing building on the Promenade in Clifton, just a few doors along from the Lord Mayor's Mansion House and fronting the Downs. There we enjoyed the honour of the patronage of Lady Somerleyton MBE JP. This august lady would turn up for special events and black and white photos show her, with smiling staff and pupils in attendance, opening various summer fairs. The school managed to produce many university entrants but on the whole the accent was on good manners and polite behaviour. At Morning Assembly we could rise as one from our hard wooden chairs without a sound. Not a scraped chair leg to be heard. Rolled-up sleeves and leaning against walls was definitely not allowed, and eating in the street positively unheard of. Few of us seemed strong on mathematics, however.

We had two extremely well-spoken Principals, Miss Bertalot (silent 't'), a concert pianist, and Miss Robinson, both of whom lived in the school. Their impressive Drawing Room, situated on the first floor, overlooked a section of the Downs called the Triangle. This was our playground and open-air theatre.

From the age of about nine I had developed a love of photography. Sadly, my very first camera was stolen from our car when we were staying in North Wales for the night en route to family in Manchester and Whitley Bay. I can see the detective now, ambling along the seafront towards our hotel, wearing a trilby and with his Mackintosh collar turned up. Very 1950s! 'This will be him,' said Dad.

It was all taken seriously, but my camera was never found and I still long for those photographs of sheep on the hills that I had taken so much trouble over. By the time I started at Duncan House in 1955 I had a Brownie camera, which gave many years of sterling service. Holidays in the Lake District, school trips and family get-togethers were all well-documented, and it is quite sweet to see how I obviously composed each shot.

I always considered photography to be artwork and now, on my travels, I mainly use my camera for future paintings. I can't remember the time when I actually stopped taking pictures as 'snaps' but specifically for use back in my studio at home. However, it definitely happened at some point along the way.

The art department in Duncan House was in a cottage across the narrow back lane, reached through the coach house arch at the back of the school garden. I have fond memories of a very blonde Miss Parminter, our young, attractive art mistress. I loved my time there and developed a liking for portraits, copying the great masters and drawing the elephant and other animals at nearby Bristol Zoo. The famous Rosie had taken us for many a bumpy ride on wooden seating with her keeper alongside. The crowds gave her pennies which she gently picked up with her trunk and then placed in her keeper's pocket. After Rosie died Wendy and Christina took her place. No big animals at the zoo now, and soon, possibly no zoo!

From my early days I had a real love of classical music, fuelled by my father's huge record collection. The great Jussi Björling singing Puccini, and Clifford Curzon's majestic interpretation of Beethoven's 4th Piano Concerto in G were among my favourites. Aged twelve I decided I would like to play the piano, and my encouraging parents bought me a Bentley piano which was installed in my bedroom. Lessons duly commenced.

The name of my first piano teacher is lost in time, but I do remember very dull lessons indeed, all scales and exercises. At home after school I had to practise for an hour a day and Dad was listening to make sure it was the whole hour. 'She wanted a piano and by Jove she was going to use it!' The hour seemed interminable. Then suddenly this little lady disappeared and the wonderful Mrs Porter arrived on the scene. From then on my lessons were a joy, and when I had my first book of proper tunes, the delightful 'Farmyard Scenes', I felt I was becoming a real pianist.

That first evening with 'Farmyard Scenes' opened I started my practice with great enthusiasm. I was really playing the piano! Suddenly a loud voice bawled out from the sitting room. 'Do your practice.'

'I am doing my practice,' I replied happily. Things were on the turn.

Eventually Miss Bertalot took over from Mrs Porter, and within two years I was playing Chopin's 'Polonaise' and other more difficult and exciting pieces, some with more notes than fingers. I didn't think anything of it at the time, but years later I met with Mrs Porter again in the Museum Art Gallery. I went straight up to her and said: 'You won't remember me Mrs Porter, but you gave me piano lessons at Duncan House.'

'I do remember you. You were so gifted I had to pass you on to Miss Bertalot.'

I was truly shocked. No one had mentioned the word 'gifted', and I certainly had never realised it. We eventually said goodbye and there were tears in my eyes as I walked down the steps out of the museum. I wish I had known.

Dad and I were Bristol Rovers supporters. Every Saturday, whatever the weather, there we were on the Eastville terraces enthusiastically watching whichever team was playing. First, Seconds, even the Colts. It was a weekend ritual, and I have to admit I was a little obsessed with the beautiful game. The Bristol City Ground was like a foreign country, and I think we only ever went once. My other teams were of course Manchester United and Newcastle United, who we regularly watched on our Northern visits. For several years I even took Charles Buchan's 'Football Monthly' and loved to draw portraits of my footballing heroes.

I was thirteen when, on the afternoon of February 6th 1958, Manchester United lost some of their most famous 'Babes' in the tragic Munich Aircrash. Duncan House used the almost-next-door Zoo Ballroom for gym and dancing lessons, and it was here on the morning after the crash a school friend broke the news. We were changing for gym and I can still feel the shock now. My mouth fell open. It couldn't be true. But of course, it was. Eight talented footballers and three United officials were lost, including the incomparable Left Half Duncan Edwards, 'Big Dunc', who won his first cap for England in April 1955 when only eighteen. How poignant that it was his portrait on the cover of the March 'Football Monthly', hot off the press, at the beginning of February 1958.

School years moved sedately on in a fairly protected and happy atmosphere. Towards my mid-teens, and then having turned a little stocky in build, I ran out of puff as a sprinter but kept goal for the school's hockey team. I was goalie for quite a few years but only because no one else would do it.

Being only a small school our rival teams were always from much larger establishments and had a greater choice of players, so we rarely won. However, I kicked away hundreds of hockey balls over the years and have the crenellated shins to prove it. The boots were sturdy enough, heavy brown leather, but shin pads, although quite large, were rather on the thin side, with white canvas over a meagre layer of horsehair.

We were taken to our various games lessons and matches in Kears Coaches. They were rather basic, noisy and rattling, but no doubt state of the art in the 1940s and 50s. Several times a week some poor soul at Kears, possibly the plump ginger-haired driver, would have had the regular job of removing clods of mud and grass from our boots that littered the coach floor.

Tennis was played on courts in the Avon Gorge and in the summer it was almost unbearable. Heat beat off the rocks onto the courts and we spent a lot of time lying down. I loved tennis though and had a very powerful hit, but unfortunately not a good sense of direction so we lost quite a few balls into the River Avon. I was quite a good ball boy, however. At that time pre-Wimbledon events were played at the Redland Tennis Courts, and one year I had the tremendous honour of ball-boying for the great Rod Laver.

The school only had one class in each year. Mine was a small and interesting group of mostly very bright students, so I felt lucky to be part of it. Cherry Rowlings was a Latin scholar, whilst my close friend Maureen Howe went on to study Medicine at the Royal Free in London. The other Maureen, Maureen Long, was a gifted pianist, and the larger-than-life Georgina Purnell, still a close friend, became a social worker. How can I forget Georgina's loud and indignant cries when she found a single pimple on her chin, just the one, when the rest of us were liberally covered? The very attractive and bubbly Susan Berry was an excellent actor and often took the lead in our many plays. She now lives in California and we still keep in touch. One of my fellow pupils was related to Russ Conway, then a very famous 'Top of the Pops' pianist. He caused a great stir when he turned up in the audience for a school concert in the Victoria Square Hall.

The Plays were important affairs and taken very seriously. Christopher Fry's *Boy with a Cart* was performed on The Triangle, our grassy playground, in front of the school. The stage in a hall on Victoria Square, Clifton Village, was used for *Androcles and the Lion, The Lady with the Lamp* and other productions in which I took only very small parts. However, in the fifth form I did have one major part in a play we wrote and produced ourselves. I don't remember much of it now other than being one half of a honeymoon couple, with my friend Stephanie, stranded in a railway station with various odd characters. It was our attempt at farce and we had lots of laughs so it must have been a success.

On reaching the Upper Sixth, Prefects and Head Girl were chosen. When the time came, the two Principals had a difficult decision to make. Our year had so many talented girls. I so hoped I would be a Prefect and was duly called in to Miss Bertalot's Drawing Room on the first floor. There it was announced by Miss

Robinson, with Miss Bertalot looking on, that I was to be Head Girl. I was genuinely shocked. The only thing I could say was, 'Golly!' It sounds so quaint now. Absolutely no one had expected that. Looking back, I am sure it was a safe choice as all the rest of the class were so ideally suited to the post. I rang my father.

'Dad, I haven't been made a Prefect.'

'Whaaat?' He sounded very disappointed.

I just hesitated slightly then said, 'I'm Head Girl!'

He was so thrilled. I can still remember the moment, with Mum cheering happily in the background.

Academically I had been a late starter and only began to settle down to work seriously by the age of fourteen. I had a lot of catching up to do. Just before my A Levels I decided to give up music and art and concentrate on academic work. I had decided on a medical career and after a disastrous result in Physics I realised I wouldn't be accepted for medicine. It hadn't crossed my or anybody else's mind to pursue art, or even music, as an actual occupation!

In 1960, after achieving only 29% in my Physics O Level, Dad decided I should have some extra tuition with gentle Mrs Wharton. She eventually became headmistress after Miss Bertalot sadly died and Miss Robinson left to marry a headmaster in Suffolk. I duly took Physics again and this time the result was a disastrous 27%! I would have to forget medicine. During my final year at school I decided to pursue a career in physiotherapy and was accepted for training at the Bristol Royal Infirmary School. Funnily enough Uncle Alan, the engineer in the family, on looking at my electrotherapy books during the Physio course, remarked that he had never seen Physics get so complicated without Maths. It was the old sums component again, my downfall at school, but I was to find I really enjoyed electrotherapy and learning all about the circuits of the machines we used for treatment.

It is so interesting to read the history of Duncan House. The school opened in 1864 with the motto 'Live to learn and learn to live'. In 1920 the great Indian poet and writer Rabindranath Tagore visited the school after hearing that girls of Duncan House had performed his play 'The King of the Dark Chamber'. The play was performed again for him and then he read one of his unpublished works. He told Miss Wilson, the much-loved headmistress of that time, that he never thought to find a school with a curriculum, method and ideals so like his own. He left with a garland of flowers made by the girls of Duncan House, and later decided to send his two nieces Monju and Joya Tagore to the school.

To this day, Miss Robinson's "Gels" still meet each year for a Reunion Lunch in Bristol.

THE NEXT FALTERING STEP

J UST BEFORE STARTING MY physiotherapy training at the Bristol
Royal Infirmary, I took a holiday job for a month at 'Hales',
the local cake factory in Clevedon. It was a rude awakening. My
introduction to the real world of work was more of a head-on
collision.

After struggling on my feet through the first day I returned
home exhausted, legs aching and half asleep. My dear Mother had
supper ready on a tray and a stool for my feet. I didn't think I could
stick it for a whole month. Although normally a cheerful soul I
was almost depressed, and the thought of a whole month in the
factory was a nightmare. But no nightmares that night. I probably
had the best sleep of my life

Not one to give in easily, I soldiered on. It was in the days before
'Health and Safety' and definitely a 'hands on' operation. Dressed
in the requisite white coat and hairnet, one of my earliest tasks
was to put tops on small drop sponges. These trundled along the
conveyor belt in rows of about five or six, already spread with jam
and some sort of cream. Doing one at a time seemed very tedious
so feeling very proud of myself for thinking it up, I held three or
four in my hand and just popped them on one after the other.
However, I was soon taken to task by the supervisor for going too

fast and possibly damaging the cakes. Well and truly put in my place, I reverted to the mind-numbing process of one at a time.

Hand washing was encouraged, and posters warned of the signs of dermatitis from handling sugar. This, hopefully, was noted by one elderly worker who, every few feet along the cake conveyor belt, would run her finger along the sides of the filled slab to remove excess jam and cream, which she then proceeded to flick, ribbon like, down the belt. She obviously found this a very satisfying experience from the look on her face. In another section snowball cakes were spread with 'cream' by hand, then dropped and rolled in a huge tub of desiccated coconut.

On one occasion I had to take loaded wooden trays of cakes on a tall trolley, from one part of the factory to another, probably from the production line to the packing room. I pushed it with great difficulty over a cobbled area, the vibrations obviously loosening the top tray, when suddenly I was nearly knocked out by the heavy wooden tray as it fell off, spilling cakes all over the cobbles. Dazed, I saw figures rushing towards me, coming to help me up, I thought. But, ignoring me with my now sore head and seeing stars, they collected up the cakes and tray, put them back on the trolley and sent me on my way.

Looking back now I see what a vital experience it was for me. I remember happy camaraderie, little time off for illness and we never heard of any food poisoning. However, I didn't eat another Hales cake, but from then on I had a great respect for factory workers.

The three-plus years training as a physiotherapist were a major step in my development. At the very beginning I watched the highly confident final-year students and was quite shocked at their tough manner and how flippant they seemed! I hoped I wouldn't become like that. However, as I was soon to find out, soft-hearted souls don't cope with the pressure of working with sick and disabled patients. Acquiring a hard shell was part of the survival process. Without it you would be unable do the job and so, naturally, I toughened up as the years passed.

Anatomy of the human body was a huge part of the course. It was the sheer amount of knowledge we had to pack into our brains as we learnt about the whole skeleton, nerves and muscles in great depth. I now realise how useful this became as my art progressed in later years.

'Three hours study a night girls, or you won't make it' we were told in very definite terms.

We were weighed down with essential text books:-*Gray's Anatomy*, *A Textbook of Medical Conditions for Physiotherapists*, *Physiotherapy in Some Surgical Conditions*, Clayton's *Electrotherapy and Actinotherapy*, Tidy's *Massage and Remedial Exercises*, and the fully illustrated *Fractures, Dislocations and Sprains*.

I was in for the long haul.

It was almost slave labour for senior students, with several patients being treated in each half hour session. As we knew nothing else we just got on with it and ploughed through our lists without any complaints from the patients. It was an excellent learning experience and I certainly don't remember long waiting lists.

One busy day during my later training and having just finished my morning list, I gave it a final check in the reception area. To my horror a new patient was about to arrive, a Lirpa Loof and needing neck traction. Well, it was going to be goodbye to lunch. New patients, with their initial assessment, always took longer to treat. The worse thing was that he or she needed neck traction, which I didn't feel confident to do on my own, and – this was the early 1960s! – there may have been language difficulties. Everyone had gone for lunch, and I needed a trained member of staff to supervise this session.

As I was quietly panicking, I heard laughing and the girls in the office appeared. It was April 1st and Lirpa Loof was, of course, April Fool backwards. I hadn't realised the date and they, longing to play a trick on someone who could take it, chose me. The relief I felt made me so grateful I couldn't be cross. I really enjoyed my lunch that day. Lunch was often bought from Mr Bull's small grocery shop opposite, usually hand-carved ham or cheese sandwiches and Mars bars! We were usually starving.

Only half of the original intake passed out in 1965. Standing on the roof of the old fracture clinic opposite the Eye Hospital we had our set photograph taken. How young and eager we all looked.

I started my professional life at the BRI working in various departments such as Short Wave, the Gym and Hydrotherapy, as well as ward work which I must admit I wasn't quite so keen on. I much preferred having control of my own department to being a small cog in a very big wheel.

In September 1966 I married local farmer John Alvis, brother of my old school friend Rachael. Sadly it was to be a mistake for both of us. We were too young and I was naïve, having had a very sheltered life at home. Dad had been too strict with me as I grew up and I was desperate to have independence and my own life. However, we had a wonderful wedding at our local church, SS Philip and Jacob in Old Market, fondly known as Pip'n'Jay. Very evangelical and soon to be a charismatic church, led by the unique Malcolm Widdecombe, it was a lively, growing congregation of committed Christians. I had made 'the commitment' myself as a student after being taken along by fellow physios. Initially, I told them I wasn't at all keen, it all sounded rather crazy, especially the young vicar. I eventually gave in. The irrepressible Malcolm and his wife Meryl became lifelong friends.

I realised there were difficulties even before we were married, but wedding plans were underway and being rather naïve then, and irresponsibly optimistic as usual, I thought it would all work out in the end. The Alvises were a lovely family, and I was generously welcomed.

John and I honeymooned in Ireland where, from our hotel, we could see a mountain that changed colour every day. It was so beautiful. We took the usual pony and trap rides and one chatty driver told us he hadn't kissed the Blarney Stone but had kissed a girl who had, which was almost the same. After a wettish week the flight home was truly awful, the plane lurching and suddenly dropping in the bad weather. After landing and with most of us rushing to the loo I heard several ladies saying 'never again'. It put me off flying for a long time.

Our married life started off in a tiny lodge cottage on Lord Wraxall's estate, Tyntesfield. It was a cosy, sweet little place and while we were here, in 1968, David was born. Soon after we moved to Castle Farm in Flax Bourton, originally the home of Lord Wraxall's agent. David's two brothers, James and Robert, soon followed. David remembers this time as the happiest of his early-childhood days. The boys could run free around the farm buildings and play together in the large tractor tyre sandpit, or on their own little tractor. Many a morning we would wake up and look over the terraced lawn to see a herd of cows, legs disappearing in the morning mist, encircling the climbing frame. They were always escaping and seemed to love congregating in that particular spot.

Later we added Becky to our family, the most darling British Alpine goat, and she was soon followed by Ben, the long-haired ginger kitten.

Around this time the Tate Gallery held an important Landseer exhibition, The Victorian artist, and Queen Victoria's favourite, Sir Edwin Landseer specialised in marvellous animal portraits. I just had to go and eventually made three visits, his work making a huge impression on me. The dogs could have 'barked', the horses 'whinnied', and the glint in their eyes so real there was always a hint of danger! A little later I took the boys on a trek around London and included a visit to the Landseer. They loved it too, and I can see the little energetic trio now, their backpacks full of lunch, walking happily for miles that day.

Before the children arrived I continued practising physiotherapy at the Bristol Royal Infirmary, and later with locum posts at Barrow Psychiatric Hospital. Rob was about fifteen months old when a friend stopped me in the sweet shop on Backwell crossroads.

'Can you do the odd day at the Children's? They are desperate and it would only be for a month or so.'

As it happened, the month or so became two years, with little Rob being looked after in the Physiotherapy department and joining in with children's treatment groups. A sensitive, musical boy, I put his compassionate nature down to this early experience with disabled children.

While working at the Bristol's Children's Hospital, James had a severe asthma attack and was admitted there as an emergency. That day he came to sit on my knee and kept whispering 'Mummy, Mummy'. He was wilting before my very eyes, and I realised this was serious. His straining chest showed the signs of a severe asthma attack. I quickly called the doctor who came straight away, and an ambulance was called, oxygen was administered, and we made a hasty trip to the Children's Hospital. As was normal then I wasn't allowed to stay, and his crying was pitiful as I left. However, each time I visited after that, he was never in bed but happily being carried around by the latest young doctor he had charmed. Such a lovely little boy, and quite brave, He would have been about four years old at the time and had been quite a sickly child, but 'on the go' day and night. 'Clinically hyperactive', I was told, but he was always very pleasant and lots of fun. One day at Castle Farm I was in the kitchen when I heard him calling out 'Mum, Mum'. I looked out of the kitchen window to see him coming down the farm track from the barns where he had been playing, a sock rolled down and plimsoll in hand. There was a hole in the top of his foot. I picked him up and took him to the sink to wash it but when I turned the foot over there was a hole in his sole as well. Off to the doctor we went, where James told him he had fallen on a piece of glass. The doctor thought how lucky he had been as it had obviously gone right through without breaking off or fracturing the bone. After a restless night he was fine. Years later he owned up to telling a lie. Despite being told never to touch the pitchforks, he was throwing one into the ground when it harpooned his foot instead. He pulled it out and concocted his story. I had always told the boys never to throw pitchforks in case that very thing happened, when they could end up losing a foot. James wasn't telling anyone the truth in case he lost his foot! Like David and Rob, James was also musical and artistic, although his overactive imagination often got the better of him. The farm cat Nicky had a good trim one morning. James decided his whiskers were much too long and untidy, so he neatened them up. Poor Nicky. Until they grew again we went through a worrying period wondering if he would get stuck somewhere, not having his proper, and of course perfect, sensory equipment. This sickly child became a rugby fanatic, eventually representing England as a student and Under-21, and spending his playing days with Newport, Pontyprydd and Exeter rugby clubs. He became a Sports Science teacher and rugby coach, but still sneezes a lot.

David the eldest was such an interesting and serious boy, with farming in his blood. He arrived as a pre-formed little man. Always talking, he was a natural scholar with a wise nature. The Alvises loved him as he was seriously interested in farming from the earliest days. Both Grandpas regularly took him to bull breeding centres, where his knowledge of prize bulls was quite impressive. He was never without his bull breeding handbook!

Rob was my only real baby. A plump cuddly little boy who just loved to quietly tag along with his brothers. He seemed to love music from an early age, and his little hands would move in time to any songs or tunes he heard. When he was crawling we had to keep a wary eye open, as Ben the ginger cat would stalk him and pounce on his neck. Many times I saw Mary, an Alvis cousin who came to babysit from time to time, beat off Ben with a rolled up newspaper! The boys were always 'the boys' and played together throughout their childhood, and without any real scraps. Rob eventually became a musician, a violin scholar at Clifton, and later a drummer in a college pop group 'Capitaan'.

So, a really mixed trio who led me a merry dance, but it was such a privilege to have them and I wouldn't have changed it for all the world. They were my joy.

When Rob was four years old we were invited to live with John's elderly relations, Uncle John and Auntie Margaret, in the picturesque family farm at Brockley Court. This was with a view to us eventually taking over the farm while, in the meantime, allowing them to enjoy their villa on the Maltese Island of Gozo.

A big family party was arranged to celebrate the 100 years of Alvis occupation of Brockley Court Farm. There was even a tree planting ceremony. The day almost didn't happen. That morning and before the great and good of the Alvis family arrived, the farmhouse was nearly a bonfire. John had so excessively banked up the fire in the heavily timbered sitting room that it set the chimney alight. The fire brigade quickly arrived, and several firemen spent hours putting the fire out before guests arrived. An exciting day all round!

The next drama was the ancient boiler. The old house with its Tudor addition had very efficient skirting heating, but every so often I would hear a loud bang and find the boiler out and with its iron door wide open. One day I actually saw the boiler blow. The iron door flew open and a sheet of flame shot out! The boiler would have to go, and, eventually, so would I.

Sadly our marriage, which had always had so many cracks from the beginning, completely fell apart at Brockley. We had moved into a nightmare scenario. This beautiful place became more like a prison, with so many rules and regulations, the boys, being so young, were confused. Play was limited and their climbing frame only allowed in the spiky shrubbery, which of course made it virtually unusable. Cycles could only be ridden and parked in certain defined places, but guns and ammunition were left around with abandon. In reality we had to be hidden from view so life could proceed as before for Aunt and Uncle. Perhaps if I had been older or more mature, I could have coped better.

The time came when I realised we had to leave. The boys were ten, eight and six years old when we moved into Bristol. My brother had kindly offered the use of his house until we were settled, so he and his lodger left, and we, plus gerbil, moved in. It became a sanctuary. We kept the house as tidy as we could, but John said he found sawdust from the gerbil cage in the carpet for many months after we left. I was so fortunate as the two Grandpas, Dick Alvis and Jack Fry, had previously decided on Clifton College for the boys. Rob was underage for the junior department, Butcombe House, but Mr Hornby, the Pre Headmaster, felt it would be best for him to join his brothers, and a long relationship with this august establishment began.

David and James came across Head of Art Peter Clay early on. David loved the exotic word games he played with them at the lunch table, but James, whom he named 'The Criminal', spent a lot of time avoiding the 'Persuader'. Peter, looking like a smaller edition of Grandpa Fry and very like him in temperament and personality, formed a happy friendship with both boys, and later, of course, with Rob.

The boys thrived at the college and especially in the Pre, where Rob was found to have a miraculous talent for the violin, eventually becoming a music scholar in the Upper School. James, primarily a sportsman, was also talented musically; he and Rob were regularly selected for the annual IAPS Orchestra. Two marvellous weeks each summer were spent at Snape Maltings with the famous conductor Sir Colin Davis, and one year, the young Nigel Kennedy.

James eventually gave the viola up, as his great love was sport and especially rugby. I immediately turned from a football fan into a rugby groupie, never quite knowing the rules but happily following his career. David, being an all-rounder, and taking his studies fairly seriously was also quite at home at Clifton and flourished there. That was until he decided he didn't like being taught Latin by rote, and from winning the Latin Prize every year he went right off the subject and his marks of course slumped. Hmm!

The boys loved Whitley Bay and with our regular visits it became, as for me, a familiar second home. Normally we went at Easter, but one summer visit especially sticks in my mind. David was spending a few weeks with a school friend, so I decided to take James and Rob to stay with Auntie Ella for a fortnight. Grandad had died and she was then living on her own in Roxburgh Terrace,

I would have to keep them busy, so I checked out the events and activities happening over those two weeks. Luckily there were daily beach competitions, and of course Beamish, the open-air museum of the North. You can't go wrong with sand and sea, so nearly every day I packed up lunch and plenty of snacks, Auntie needing something to eat every two hours or low blood sugar would bring on the grumps. Off we all went to the beach. One day it was Whitley Bay, the next Cullercoats and then Tynemouth. Each had a different activity, treasure hunts, races and sandcastle competitions with prizes of large bars of Cadbury's Milk Tray. We entered them all. James's submarine won one sandcastle competition and Rob's extensive castle complex another. Rob, who finds everything, won the treasure hunts and both boys managed to win races. I was beginning to feel a little awkward, turning up each day and wondering if other parents were thinking 'Oh, no, not those boys again!' Time for a change.

Beamish is a great place to visit and then, even it is early days, provided lots of entertainment and historical interest. There were old Northumbrian streets and shops, vehicles and crafts, but on that day the boys were a real handful. As Dad used to say, 'they've got it on them'. They raced around making nuisances of themselves, climbing where they shouldn't, and after finding a large peacock feather kept tickling each other. Other groups of children seemed to be so well behaved, and I wondered if parents were looking on disapprovingly.. We would have to leave, but suddenly we came across a tent and inside a lady in traditional dress sitting at her spinning wheel. It was like a miracle. Both boys sat cross-legged, quite mesmerised, and just watched. Oh, the relief. Auntie and I went off for a coffee, and when we came back they were still there.

On our last day I decided to visit a raspberry farm further up in Northumberland. We could pick raspberries to take home and some to leave with Auntie. It was a lovely sunny day and as we parked near the entrance to the field, I said to Auntie, 'Will you come with us?' No, she would prefer to say in the car. Off we went and at a leisurely pace, filled several punnets, the boys eating their way round. We paid at the booth and got back in the car.

Auntie looked cross. 'Where have you been? Picking your own?'

'Yes Auntie, it is a Pick Your Own farm. There's the large notice!' We had to laugh.

Prior to leaving Brockley and after several locum duties, Barrow Psychiatric Hospital Physiotherapy department offered me a position, but were unable to let me have school holidays off. This had been at the most difficult time for me, when I needed a break from the confines of Brockley Court Farm. Unable to take the position at Barrow, with no one to look after the children during their long holidays, my father offered me a job, with school holidays free, in his latest business, Wessex Sales Organisation. This was his next and final venture after the newspaper shops. Here he specialised in selling Sub-Post Office attached businesses, after owning Henleaze Post Office. He had found the process of actually buying it, then provided by ordinary estate agents, quite inadequate. It needed the specialist handling he eventually offered, and he soon becoming a leading agent in this field.

After being trained up by Dad, and right out of the blue, I received another offer of work from Barrow Hospital, this time with school holidays off. It really was with some sadness and great regret that I had to turn down this wonderful offer. By then I felt duty bound to my father, who was relying on me for all advertising, as well as actually visiting Post Office businesses around the country. My territory ranged from Manchester to Bournemouth, and I enjoyed driving, meeting the Sub-Postmasters and assessing their businesses. It was in the days before mobile phones which made for pleasant travelling, but with, of course, plenty of work piling up back at the office. Wessex Sales Organisation also provided a questionnaire service for businesses nationwide, and some days quite a batch arrived on my desk. Sub-Postmasters had to be telephoned, selling price agreed, then the business well written up prior to marketing. I managed it, but seemed to be running all the time just to catch up.

In May 1985, at the age of only 62, my poor father was diagnosed with terminal liver cancer. Looking back, he had aged during the previous year, his face becoming more lined, although still very handsome and full of life. After his initial shock and depression he was so brave, living life to the full as long as he could. We managed to keep him going for six months until 20th December. It seemed surprisingly quick at the end. One minute joking with the nurses in Clevedon Cottage Hospital, and the next, just dying. It all seemed so surreal. Where was he? He had been the centre of all our lives.

My boys felt the loss very badly. Grandpa was the one who took them boating, shared their holidays in Whitley Bay, supported them when they played cricket and rugby, and turned up at all the concerts. He bought their first bikes and Rob his violin. Decades later, James still has trouble talking about his adored Grandpa without crying. When his second child was born, the name 'Jack' was chosen. During the Christening party, James made his speech. Right at the beginning, as he started to say why Jack was so called, he choked up and couldn't go on. Mary, his wife, had to finish for him. A photograph shows family and friends, glasses in hand ready to toast the little boy, all with such sympathy on their faces. He was so cross with himself. Normally never lost for words and an excellent speech maker, this one was too painful for him. He blurted out, 'I had so much to say, too.'

Following Dad's death, with Mother very bereaved and the business to continue, pressures on me were enormous. Suddenly I found myself doing the work of three people. Dad's position as head of the firm had to be filled, as well as that of our 'rep' Alec who had only recently resigned through ill health, and on top I had my own work. I was still a mother of three teenage boys, so tackling four jobs I suppose. I managed to hold Wessex together successfully for three years, until a severe case of flu laid me low in the early spring of 1988. After a couple of days off work I soldiered on, but never quite recovered. Severe, debilitating migraines and flu-like symptoms were to dog me from then on, and I was diagnosed as having ME, the controversial myeloencephalitis.

I found this difficult to understand at the time, but looking back now I see how ridiculous this workload was, and my body simply refused to put up with it. After the initial illness I had years of reduced stamina, rarely feeling well and, to this day, although the symptoms have at last faded, I still have to be careful not to take on too much. It had taken nearly 20 years to recover, losing my prime, which could be looked on as a terrible waste of a life, but on the other hand it allowed me the privilege of developing as an artist. Twenty years is a lot of life to lose, and at the time I felt quite confused and embarrassed about the illness, and especially as it was known in the Press as 'yuppy flu'. All I knew was that my mental and physical energy had gone, my muscles ached, my legs frequently gave way and my food tasted different, rather metallic. Compared to many with a similar condition I had great support from my own doctor, Valerie Peet. She knew me well and that the last thing I wanted was to be laid up as life passed me by. She sent me to a virus specialist at Frenchay Hospital, the wonderful

Dr Stuart Glover. I then had strong medication for the migraine which helped at times, and more than anything I had the support of medics who knew I was suffering from something real and debilitating.

There was no short-term recovery. I just had to weather it, but as the years passed by my life slowly improved.

In the very early days I found a respite from the illness by taking up lace making. I loved the quiet companionship of fellow lace makers at our weekly meetings, conveniently held at Redland Training College just a few minutes' walk away and here I immersed myself in the gentle pleasure of a day's lacemaking. My cousin Bill's wife Alex, a doctor, was also a brilliant and very gifted lacemaker who encouraged me as I slowly developed this intricate skill. We began taking 'lacing holidays' together, often with weekends at Springetts of Rugby and a week each November with lace makers from all over the country at the Imperial Hotel in Exmouth. I found it to be a very therapeutic and fulfilling pastime. As opposed to painting which, when it took over my life, became more of a demanding 'drive' and not at all therapeutic! I had always enjoyed drawing and painting in a small way, but I was soon to be completely taken over by it and my lace making slowly diminished to become a happy memory. It was in the late 1980s when I met Peter Clay at the Royal West of England Academy. The lace pillow was put aside.

TRAVELS 1988-1993

M Y LOVE OF TRAVEL must have come about because of Saturday morning visits to The Vandyke Cinema in Fishponds. How I loved Shirley Temple, Flash Gordon and tales of the old Wild West with 'cowboys and Indians', Hopalong Cassidy and Roy Rogers. I was especially fascinated by Native American Indian life and tales of other exotic cultures.

It was 1988 and I was sitting at the kitchen table, with sunlight streaming in through the window, thinking there must be more to my life than this. Confined to home much of the time with the world passing me by, I definitely needed a change.

Glasgow (1988)

An advert in the Bristol Evening Post caught my eye. A weekend coach trip to the Glasgow Garden Festival. It seemed a rather lovely opportunity and we would surely be travelling with a group of gentle horticulturists. I had taken trouble planning and developing my little garden in Beaconsfield Road, so this was the ideal time to see what was happening in the larger gardening world. Mum, still missing Dad, of course, was up for it, and so we booked our seats straightaway. This minor trip became my introduction to world travelling.

I don't think there was a single serious gardener on board the bus! We had come away with a very jolly Bingo group from Kingswood. Throughout the long journey we were regularly entertained by various renditions on the spoons by a gentleman who was quite the expert. Halfway to Glasgow the coach driver, in playful mood, told us all to look at the view behind us.

'Hanham Mount!' he exclaimed. The group, some from Kingswood and some from adjoining Hanham, loved it. Hanham Mount was where George Whitefield and John Wesley had preached to the miners of Kingswood in the mid-1700s. John Wesley is reputed to have said that the miners of Kingswood were a wild and ungovernable bunch. I suddenly thought of gentle Auntie Em and her smallholding in Cock Road. However, in the late 18th century the Cock Road Gang terrorised the Kingswood area with horse stealing, highway robbery and protection rackets! A member of their gang was a Fry, a relation of ours no doubt!

As we approached Glasgow the weather turned against us, and our weekend was very wet and exceptionally windy. Arriving at the Garden Festival, wondering whether we were the only ones of the group to actually visit, we had to cross Bell Bridge. This was nigh impossible. The wind had reached gale force and, clinging together, Mum and I just managed to make it across, but it took quite a while. Sadly there is little else to remember from that weekend but, most importantly, it opened the door to future travels.

New York (1989)

On Saturday 7th October 1989 I opened the arts section of the weekend *Daily Telegraph* where staring me in the face was a quite marvellous and mesmerising portrait. Surely, here was a bitter, intelligent and aristocratic man, and all this could be read in the painting. The artist was obviously a genius. I wanted to find out more.

The article, by Richard Dorment, described a major exhibition of paintings by the great Spanish artist Velazquez. Born in 1599, his portrayals were so fresh and honest they almost spoke. This unique exhibition was at the Metropolitan Museum of Art, New York, and only until 7th January. I had to go.

'Mum, will you come to an exhibition with me?' I asked, giving her a cup of coffee.

She looked unenthusiastic. 'Oh, we aren't going to London again, are we?'

I had dragged her along to many exhibitions in London galleries over the years. Not that she hadn't enjoyed most of them, it was just the effort of getting to London on the train as I no longer wanted to drive and indeed now had no car.

'No.' She looked reassured and luckily put her coffee down.

'New York.'

Mum fell back on the sofa.

Early that December there we were, at Gatwick Airport, boarding a Virgin plane for one of their Christmas shopping specials: five nights in a central hotel, transfers, plus a sightseeing trip around New York all thrown in. It was exciting, but terrifying at the same time. Land travel was my thing. I wasn't too keen on flying after that most uncomfortable, lurching flight from Cork to Bristol back in 1966. However, the draw of the Velasquez exhibition took me over, and so this would be my first long haul flight. I found myself nervously walking down the corridor to the plane, chewing a toffee very vigorously.

As it turned out, we had a most uneventful and pleasant flight and duly arrived safely in the USA. Included in the Virgin itinerary was a trip around New York City, and we sat in the coach rather starstruck as locations for West Side Story were pointed out, then the iconic Flat Iron building, Chinatown and the harbour with the Statue of Liberty in the distance. We couldn't wait to explore. Mum was loving it.

New York was wonderful. How we loved the tall buildings, the bustle and pace. Father Christmases rang bells on the sidewalks between the steam plumes we had seen so many times on old American movies. We lingered by famous stores on Fifth Avenue, gazing at their fantastic window displays. Skaters whizzed and pirouetted at the Rockefeller Center ice rink, and, at night, the trees twinkled with tiny white lights. It was a magical experience.

Our first visit to the imposing Metropolitan Museum of Art was awe-inspiring, and the Velasquez exhibition was all that Richard Dorment had described. But for me, the greater revelation was of American artists I had not known before, and especially Winslow Homer. His pictures looked as if they could have been painted last week, instead of last century.

I was thrilled to find Homer had visited Cullercoats in the North East of England – that beautiful little horseshoe beach between Whitley Bay and Tynemouth. His painting of 'Fisher Girls on the Beach at Cullercoats' now hangs in the Brooklyn Museum. The row of little fishermen's cottages he had seen, as indeed had I in the 1950s, was demolished in the 1960s. What lack of foresight! I remember so well the fisherwomen in their doorways, dressed in black, with shawls wrapped round their shoulders, selling fish that would have been caught that very morning. In their place now are flats and town houses, surely reducing Cullercoats to another seaside suburb, except of course for that lovely little beach with its steep slipway from the lifeboat house down to the water's edge.

Just around the corner from our hotel in New York was the magnificent Museum of Modern Art, MoMA. Here the draw of the season was 'Pioneering Cubism by Picasso and Braque'. It was a huge and thrilling exhibition which managed to convey the excitement and drive of both artists as they visited each other's studio each night to see what the other had accomplished that day. Mum refused to go in, but sat happily in the busy foyer watching the world and his wife come and go. 'I'm not paying seven dollars to see that rubbish!'

Of course, we managed to fit in some Christmas shopping. Using Mum for sizing, her head being bigger than mine, I bought a 'Connecticut Crusher' hat for David. She was beginning to get a little fed up with trying on lots of hats, spoiling her hair!

A trip to Staten island on the Ferry was a 'must', and a photograph shows Mum chatting animatedly with a very good-looking policeman! Then, one night, up we went to the viewing platform of the Empire State Building where we gazed in wonder at New York in all its illuminated glory. How poignant now, remembering a clear sunny day when we were propelled by express elevator to the top of the Twin Towers. From there we could see right across to Connecticut and, looking way down, at small planes as they flew below us. On another sunny day, twelve years later, the world would watch in horror as terrorists reduced the Twin Towers to rubble.

Later moved by the first President Bush to a more important site in Washington, the Museum of the American Indian was then part of a university complex in Spanish Harlem. Having this lifelong fascination with other cultures, and especially Native American Indians, it was an essential visit for me. I thought back to those rowdy Saturday mornings at the Vandyke Cinema in Fishponds, the poor manager appearing on stage several times each week, threatening to end the show if we didn't quieten down!

As we progressed north on the subway towards Harlem, we realised we were entering the poorer and more threatening outskirts of the city. We sat quietly on the train holding our shopping bags containing city maps on our laps, hoping we would appear to be locals. We eventually arrived, stepped out onto the platform over a few prostrate bodies, hopefully still alive, and made our way out into the sunshine. On that day my Mother and I, together with a young black family and a German backpacker, were the only visitors to this marvellous museum. We met the backpacker in the photographic gallery.

'Vat does "paraphernalia" mean?' he asked me as we looked at wonderful black and white photographs of itinerant Native Americans.

'Their worldly goods and belongings, "bits and pieces"', I answered, and he nodded gratefully. Although we stayed in the museum for quite a long time, we saw no other visitors. By then our short stay in New York was about to end, but it had been such an enriching and unforgettable experience.

This memorable trip was the beginning of a new chapter in my life. My first taste of serious travel, leading the way to exotic locations and cultures that would inspire my paintings from then on.

South Africa (1990)

In the summer of 1989 James left for South Africa. Having just finished A Levels at Clifton he was to spend a year as 'dogsbody', the official title being Junior Housemaster, at Bishop's Diocesan College in Cape Town. This was his gap year prior to training in Sports Science at Cardiff Institute. It was all arranged by the Clifton Pre Headmaster, Roger Trafford. The connection was the Headmaster of Bishop's Prep School who had been Roger's best man, and he needed 'Three Stooges', as he put it. I prayed James would stick it and not get homesick, as I knew he would pack up and come home if he wasn't happy.

True to form, James packed all his worldly goods in Uncle John's old school trunk which was then shipped to the Cape. He couldn't possibly be without the security of all his important bits and pieces, his 'paraphernalia'. Memories arose of his 'private box' that, as a young child, he carried at all times. A square brown

45rpm record box with a black handle, it was full of his little treasures, and we weren't allowed to look inside.

Mum and I saw him off from Heathrow airport on a sunny June day. 'If anything happens to me,' he said, 'I want to have my funeral service in the College Chapel'. A great note to leave me with, I must say!

Arriving in Cape Town in the middle of a rainy, wintry June, James was immediately homesick. Missing home and friends, letters arrived from him counting the days and hours until his return. I had visions of him packing up and leaving, and quite soon too! Not wanting the embarrassment – and it cost quite a bit to send the trunk - I assured him that Gran and I would visit when we could. He seemed to settle.

A South African friend put us in touch with 'Friends of the Springbok' who helped organise a month-long trip for the following March. With James' instructions to be obeyed, it was a rather complicated and full itinerary.

In 1990 South African Airways was not allowed to fly over the continent of Africa so we had to follow a coastal route, the journey taking twelve hours. It was a pleasant enough flight, and as we prepared to land we gazed open-mouthed at the beauty of the Cape. I had never seen anything like it. It looked like paradise.

What we didn't know was that wind currents over the Cape could make landings difficult. As we touched down the plane tilted over to the right so much we thought it wouldn't recover. It was a very strange and frightening sensation. There were murmurings of great relief all round when we eventually righted and came to a halt. As we disembarked the warmth of the sun seemed to envelop us in a comforting blanket. We all turned our faces up gratefully to meet it. Entering the terminal, though, we were conscious of anxious faces.

'We thought you were tipping right over,' exclaimed a happy but tearful James. The landing had obviously been a frightening sight, but we were safely there and our African experience was about to begin.

Mum and I were so thrilled to see James again. In cricket whites he looked fit, tanned and handsome, his fair hair bleached by the African sun. After hugs and tears we were quickly whisked away to 'Bishops' where James was in the middle of umpiring an end-of-term match between masters and boys. It felt unreal. One minute in a plane and the next in the middle of a very English tableau, watching cricket and having tea but, exotically, under the shadow of Table Mountain.

James had decided for us that the Newlands Sun Hotel was the place to stay and use as a base. Newlands, that leafy suburb, home of famous cricket and rugby grounds, and most importantly for him, close to the school in Rondebosch, was a perfect choice. Especially as he was thinking of joining us for breakfasts! We were within site of Table Mountain and around round the corner from the hotel was a small local station from where we could reach the centre of Cape Town in minutes. It was all so exotic and exciting.

One morning when James arrived for breakfast, he announced he wasn't feeling too well. Could he lie down on one of the beds for a while? That was fine of course but soon there was a knock at the door. A tall young waiter arrived with the tea James had obviously ordered on his arrival. The young man, tray in hand, looked across to see this tanned blond youth in one of the beds with two, supposedly respectable, older ladies looking on. His hesitation was only momentary, and his eyebrows raised only a millimetre or two, as he put down the tray and quickly retreated. I am sure the rest of the staff, who knew us all by then, would have explained the situation to him but the shock obviously cured James immediately. Red-faced, he hurriedly got up and we all went down for breakfast.

We loved the school and as he escorted us there James was immediately surrounded by boys, clinging to him like bees around a honeypot. He had become rather a hero, especially after one notable cricket match when he scored a six. Not only did the ball leave the pitch but entered the only open window halfway up a neighbouring block of flats. Rushing up to apologise and retrieve the ball, James found an elderly lady having tea. Fortunately for him she didn't seem too upset, just rather surprised.

Parents as well as boys seemed to appreciate James's stay at Bishops, and one evening we were invited to dine at the Coconut Grove Club. It was a lovely occasion with generous hosts, so typical of our stay in Cape Town and indeed, as we were to find throughout South Africa.

The Cape has to be one of the most beautiful places on earth. A true paradise, but one with a difficult history. We arrived in the year Nelson Mandela was at last released from Robben Island. Remnants of privileges for whites were all too obvious. In the local train station signs still declared 'Whites Only', and it was unusual to find white people in any area of service. Back home many felt it was not yet politically correct to visit South Africa, but I am so glad we did. We met and were welcomed by many wonderful South Africans, black, white, and 'coloured' as mixed race peoples are known there. They were mostly excited, yet apprehensive for the future of their beautiful land. South Africa was on the very cusp of change.

'Nelson Mandela doesn't speak for all of us, you know,' declared a Zulu taxi driver. This brought home James's experience. The only racial problems he encountered in school were not between black and white boys, but between black boys from different tribes. There were many different tribes as well as the English Whites, Afrikaans and mixed-race communities. I was soon to realise that a short holiday doesn't make an expert on this complex country. Best to keep quiet, observe and learn.

Glorious Cape Town, with the beautiful park gardens of Governors Walk, its superb museums and art galleries, was, in fact, a show piece, and so very clean. After our first day out we came back to the hotel in Newlands and washed our hands ready for dinner.

The water running off our hands was as clean as that coming out of the tap. Definitely a first.

We learnt to appreciate artists and sculptors who were all quite new to us. The bronzes of van Wouw were especially masterly, and the paintings of Laubser and Pierneef an absolute joy. There were many examples of grandfather clocks and Cape Dutch furniture made with gorgeous woods such as stinkwood and yellow wood. A delight to the senses, as was the Cape air, perfumed with the scent of frangipani, a shrub used as hedging and as common as our privet.

Our stay in Cape Town was a mix of essential sightseeing and, of course, rugby.

We enjoyed being temporary supporters of Cape Villagers Rugby Club. It was the Cape's short autumn but still very hot for the game by our standards, and watching clouds of red dust billowing up as the lads stampeded around the ground was quite something to behold.

What with his rugby matches and training it was difficult to pin James down, but we managed it, although not without some insistence on my part. Visiting the old fishing town of Hout Bay we carried on to the Cape of Good Hope via Chapman's Peak, one of the world's most spectacular scenic drives. At Cape Point the Atlantic meets the Indian Ocean, and a signpost points to the world's major cities. We looked eastwards, thinking of Rob. He had chosen to do his Sixth Form studies at Wells Cathedral School where he had been accepted into the specialist music unit, and was, at that very time, touring Hong Kong and Malaysia with the school's Chamber Orchestra.

One warm evening we took the cable car to the top of Table Mountain. It was bathed in a golden red light, and as the day slipped away we watched the lights of Cape Town sparkling below us. It was so peaceful and all we could hear was the squeaking of the rock hyrax, or 'dassies', scampering from rock to rock. It really seemed as if all the wonders of nature were concentrated in this magical place.

An obligatory tour of Groot Constantia and wine tasting was planned by James, and on another day we, or rather I, drove miles out to a rather remote and barren coastal area to find an oyster restaurant. He tucked in!

Our booking had included use of a rental car, but on collecting it we found James, being under 21, was not allowed to drive. This was despite the fact that he was transporting boys in the school bus on a regular basis. He was not at all pleased.

A day trip to nearby Stellenbosch was planned. Mum and I drove out to this picturesque town, the second oldest in South Africa, and were immediately charmed by its character. Dating from the 1660's, it is a living museum with oak tree lined streets and examples of houses from each era in its history. It was here in a small gallery I came across the naïve but powerful paintings of Maggie Laubser. I bought a print of a mother, surrounded by sheep, with a child bound to her back. I wasn't sure at the time, but the gallery owner said I would regret not having it - and she was right. I love it still. Before we left Stellenbosch we found Oom Samie se Winkel - 'Uncle Sammy's Shop' - the most memorable building in town. As we entered its crammed emporium a heady mix of aromas overwhelmed us. Tobacco, soap, coffee and biltong of course. This historic old trading store was an amazing and unusual experience.

The day was so very hot and I photographed a turkey, underneath an oak tree, wisely trying to cool down by standing in a small tin bath of water.

We got lost on the drive back to our hotel in Newlands. It was a milky dusk and very difficult to see road markings and signs. Unexpectedly arriving at a township, I had to stop ask the way. An old lady ran out of her shack to help. She looked anxious as she told us how to get back to Cape Town. I often wonder if the area was one we shouldn't have entered.

A fellow Clifton pupil and friend of James, Jeremy Cansdale, was working in a church school to the north of the country. We had arranged to meet up in the Cape and together tour part of the Garden Route area. Jeremy eventually arrived after a very long and squashed trip in a black taxi. We set off together for the Little Karoo to visit Cango crocodile farm and famous caves, then on to Highgate Ostrich Farm, 'The Feather Capital of the World', in Oudtshorn. It had to be this farm, as it was here Jeremy's father Michael, in his youth, had also ridden an ostrich. I later learnt the eminent heart surgeon, Professor Christian Barnard, had also ridden an ostrich at Highgate.

But first, we were shown around a crocodile farm by an elderly man with only one arm. We wondered if a croc had got him. The boys loved it but were less keen to include a visit to the Cango Caves. I insisted, and have a photo of them standing there rather dejectedly, chewing on biltong. The caves were in fact quite spectacular and included realistic tableaux of the original Hottentot inhabitants, as well as a reference to Cheddar Caves of all places!

Perked up by the biltong, the boys' spirits improved and we set off for the ostrich farm. They were not disappointed and duly rode the ostriches, did the obligatory stand on eggs to prove they would not break, and watched ostrich races. It was fun, but so very hot and dry. Finally we bought our ostrich feather dusters, laughed at some meerkats, then, after goodbyes to Jeremy, made for our last destination of George, and the Carmel Christian Holiday Camp. Situated on a wooded mountainside, in sight of Victoria Bay and the famous Outeniqua 'Choo Tjoe', within easy reach of Knysna and Wilderness lagoons, Carmel was a perfect retreat.

Jeremy had suggested we visit Carmel and had arranged a short stay for us. Mum was a little hesitant and wondered if it was going to be "very 'Christian'!" It turned out to be the most peaceful and loving place for families of all races to enjoy a holiday. We had such a generous welcome and no pressure to do anything but just 'be', and take part in as much, or none, of the activities as we chose.

On arrival we signed in at the office where, with other items for sale, I saw a small stone with a tiny stick insect on top. It was a lovely thing and I thought 'I must buy that'. Luckily I didn't say anything. When I peered down to look more closely, the stick insect slowly moved its head. This was Africa and it was, of course, alive. I purchased a flannel with the Carmel logo on instead.

Mum and I were taken into what seemed like a suite, whereas James had the use of a rickety old caravan in the grounds. What we didn't realise at the time was that Carmel had been full and a family had vacated their suite especially for us. They would have booked this accommodation months, if not a year, before, and yet, without a murmur, we were given it for our three-day stay. What generosity, and so typical of the welcome we found all over South Africa.

However, James was less appreciative. Keeping amazingly cheerful despite the thought of massive spiders and other wildlife joining him through gaps in the caravan and its ill-fitting door, he hung all his belongings from the ceiling and gave his shoes a good shake each morning.

The communal meals were lively and friendly, and at breakfast we were introduced to mealy porridge, a tasty staple. One day a picnic was arranged at the nearby Wilderness Lagoon board walk and it seemed as if everyone was going, so off we went too. It turned out to be a wonderful affair on a glorious blue day. Out came the tables and tablecloths, china cups and plates, like an old-fashioned English village tea party. Here I met Margy Cowell, who was on furlough from missionary work in Mozambique. We walked along the board walk together as she pointed out various birds and their distinguishing songs. What a sweet, hardworking lady she was. We enjoyed her gentle company and have kept in touch ever since. Margy's prayer letters arrive fairly regularly from Mozambique and more recently from South Africa, keeping us up to date with her work. It is humbling to know of hardships experienced with courage and cheerfulness by the people of that country, and those like Margy who serve them with such dedication.

We left Carmel refreshed and uplifted. Often in our minds' eyes we are back in their fragrant grounds looking over the wooded valley and down to little Victoria Bay, with the sight and sound of the 'Choo Tjoe' train chugging and puffing along below us.

Jeremy had returned north and we made our way back to Cape Town via Plettenberg Bay. In 1576 the Portuguese explorer Mesquita da Perestelo named the area Bahia Formosa – Beautiful Bay. It was settled in 1630 by shipwrecked sailors from Europe and later named Plettenberg after a Governor of the Cape, Joachim van Plettenberg. It is a spectacular and sought-after resort, said to enjoy 320 days of sunshine each year, with an expanse of sea where dolphins love to play with surfers.

The headmaster of Bishops, Mervyn Grey, and his family, together with fellow teachers Ed and Willow Milne, had holiday homes beautifully situated overlooking the bay, and we were invited to join them for meals and more sightseeing. Ed took us to the actual shore where the first Portuguese had landed way back in the 16th century. To the Milnes' great amusement, we were genuinely surprised to find a grapefruit tree in their garden, absolutely laden with huge yellow fruit. Nothing unusual for them, but a first for us!

On our return to the Cape there were more rugby matches to watch before travelling on to Johannesburg. James planned to join us for a few days' safari before returning to Bishops in time for the new term. We were staying on in Johannesburg before flying home from Jan Smuts airport.

Originally planning to travel on the Blue Train for the two-day journey from Cape Town to Johannesburg, we were disappointed to find it was fully booked. So we left it, hoping there might be a cancellation on the day. We were lucky. After a few hours in the

Blue Train office, a cancellation was found. The only vacancy was a cabin for three which we gratefully paid for and, after profuse thanks to the diligent clerk, we went out into the Cape sunshine to enjoy the rest of our stay.

Later, on board the train, we were escorted to our cabin to await the attention of the manager. Staff were constantly polishing inside and out, and we felt rather grand as we admired our home for the next two days and opened the welcoming champagne. The manager arrived, took one look at the size of James and announced he was to be given his own cabin. So, off James went to this, amazingly free, cabin. The next we saw of him he was looking for all the world quite at home, leaning back on the commodious berth, sipping his own champagne! We met up with him later in the plush lounge bar with its exotic floral displays as we travelled north on one of the world's greatest train journeys.

Leaving Cape Town and the fertile Hex River Valley we soon entered the semi-arid Little Karoo and then the harsher central Karoo, with a short stop in Matjiesfontein opposite the elegant Lord Milner Hotel. Built in the 19th century by a young Scot, James Douglas Logan, the hotel was used as a hospital for British officers during the Boer War. It seemed quite incongruous, a luxurious, very British-looking hotel in the middle of a South African desert.

Passing through the diamond producing Kimberley area and vast plains of sunflowers, we eventually reached the gold mining centre of Klerksdorp in the Western Transvaal, and here we enjoyed a welcome stretch of legs on the platform.

We were soon to arrive in the golden city of Johannesburg, but the memory of that unique journey is still imprinted in my mind. The food was spectacular, and it was here I had my first and only taste of crumbed crocodile tail! It was actually quite delicious and not unlike a fishy chicken. We met such interesting fellow travellers, and especially one, a very wealthy Afrikaans farmer with his young son. He obviously regularly rode the Blue Train and was well known – and very well served by the staff. Our meeting was fortunate as he recommended we visit Haia Safari. Here we would find authentic tribal dancing, an experience not to be missed.

On our arrival, the next step of our journey was to take the short Comair flight to Skukuza airport for a three-day safari at Sabi Sabi. Alongside the Kruger National Park and deep in the bush, Skukuza was no more than an airstrip surrounded by thatched buildings and a tree-lined path giving welcome shade. A jeep arrived and we were transported to Sabi Sabi Game Reserve. The heat was intense and the air so dry and dusty, it was a most unusual experience. On arrival at the lodge reception a female porter took my heavy suitcase, and with impressive speed and accuracy deftly placed it on her head and led the way to our accommodation with such determination I didn't have time to say 'I can do it'.

Walking to our thatched rondavel chalet, we were startled by the cries of a woman in obvious distress. A large praying mantis had fallen out of the thatch onto her head. A nice start to her holiday for the poor woman. It couldn't have been too pleasant for the mantis either, as it sat in the dust slowly moving its head from side to side.

Visiting the small encampment shop we purchased suitable safari gear, khaki shirts, t-shirts and shorts to keep us inconspicuous on the drives. It was the end of the season so not much choice, but items were on sale. It was exciting nevertheless, and we definitely didn't want to stand out in the bush. No pink t-shirts to scare the animals or let them think we were lunch.

'Helloooo!' We were greeted by the young assistant in the soft sing-song voice so typical of the black South Africans. He smiled and helped us with the appropriate sizes.

We slipped easily into safari routine. Rising each dawn for tea, and the delicious sweet rusk biscuit so popular in South Africa, we set off on our drives. With six in a jeep, including our armed African tracker and a ranger, we bumped over the dusty ground and met the morning light with great anticipation. Holding on for dear life and regularly ducking to avoid the acacia bushes and their vicious eye-level spines, we searched expectantly for game. Keeping very quiet we watched groups of impala hiding in the bush, and herds of wildebeest continually grazing and making their distinctive grunting sound. A mother warthog with her two babies ran squealing ahead of us, their little tails pointing skywards. A pride of lions sloped leisurely across our path, and a family of curious cheetahs seemed to want to join us. On one occasion these gorgeous animals were just lying lazily on the dirt track under trees, beginning to feel the heat of the approaching day, when, in a split second, they were up and running like lightning, chasing an unlucky impala with impressive speed. I am glad to say we didn't see the actual deed.

Passing huge red termite mounds, a velvet-coated giraffe loped by, and in the bush a well camouflaged rhinoceros silently watched us. Monkeys chased and played in the trees, but were deemed a nuisance in the camp. We were warned not to share our morning rusks with them, or they would be shot!

It was incredibly hot during the day and after the morning drive, we spent our time swimming in the small, semi-shaded pool and resting under whirring fans in our rondavel.

The evening drives began in the early dusk and by seven o'clock it was fully dark, offering a most wonderful opportunity to see the elusive leopard and hornbills dramatically silhouetted against the evening sky. At the end of the drive, and still in the bush, the jeeps stopped. Out came the drinks and we had our 'sundowners' under a sky absolutely crammed with stars. 'Aah...' we cried, as shooting stars crossed the heavens.

Nights were anything but quiet. Crickets chirped constantly, mosquitoes buzzed and every so often we could hear the loud roar of a lion. It struck home in an instant. Back in Bristol I often heard lions in nearby Clifton Zoo, but this was the real thing! We were warned never to walk out at night.

One morning we found a trail of huge round footprints outside. 'Hippos', said our quiet, smiling friend in the shop, 'making their way from the Sabie River into the bush.' To think, they had lumbered by as we slept, and we hadn't heard a thing.

On one evening drive we walked down a small bank to the river where hippos were swimming. Our ranger walked in front whilst the tracker stayed watchfully behind. A sudden crashing sound made us all jump, and out of the bush came our tracker who had just come face to face with a leopard! Both were startled. Just prior to that, our ranger had seen a large Cape buffalo nearby. The most dangerous of animals, it was easily roused. If it decided to charge it would be difficult to escape, and almost impossible to shoot because of the massive horn formation across the front of its head. So here we were in the bush, down a steep slope and between two dangerous animals.

'Time to leave,' said Ranger. 'Quick as you like!'. Mum, who always maintained she couldn't walk quickly, was up that slope and into the jeep with lightning speed, legs going like pistons!

Evenings at Sabi Sabi were a sociable affair with barbecues around the fire in the enclosed Boma and everyone discussing their sightings of the day. Here we sampled roast ostrich which tasted rather like a tough turkey to me, but perhaps it had been a little too long on the braai.

I picked up a magazine called 'Getaway' with a feature on Sabi Sabi. Altogether a fascinating read on South African holidays in general, it had the most interesting section on outdoor camping. South Africans love their sausage, the *boerewors*, and here was a recipe to make the biggest sausage of all time. Entitled, 'For the Very Hungry' and prepared for a festival, the ingredients included 17 cattle, 14 bacon pigs, 1000kg potatoes, 60kg salt, 60kg spices and mixed herbs, 100kg sausage skin and 100 litres of vinegar. After three days of preparation and cooking, the giant sausage was carried by means of a crane and truck to the braai where it was cut into more manageable lengths.

Our few days at Sabi Sabi passed all too quickly and we were soon back at Skukuza awaiting our small plane to Johannesburg. My only disappointment was the lack of elephants. We had seen evidence of their passing through, but they move so quickly over great distances and had chosen that very time to be somewhere else. I love these animals and badly wanted to see them, but have to admit with some embarrassment that after a fairly extensive trip to Africa, the only elephant I saw was in Johannesburg Zoo.

Our time in Sabi Sabi had been an interesting lesson in wildlife photography. It was very difficult! Game drives were in mostly subdued light; animals were either camouflaged or moving, and so images were never as good as expected. Luckily I managed a few 'gems' which I could use back home. My admiration soars for the professional, and of course BBC wildlife photographers.

Our hotel in Johannesburg was the downtown Holiday Inn. Chosen at a distance from the comfort of home because it had a pool, we couldn't have known how close it was to the more unsavoury districts of the city. On our very first day we saw a plume of dark smoke rising high in the air just a short distance away. This was from a 'necklacing' on the nearby railway line. This most awful 'punishment' was to place a car tyre around a victim's neck and set it alight.

James wanted to ring friends in the UK from his hotel room but we said, 'Certainly not. It will be much too expensive.' So, off he went in a huff to his own room. A little later we left our room and further down the hall passed a couple of trays on the floor with remnants of what had obviously been a very good meal.

'Someone's been enjoying themselves,' said Mum as we went out to look at the shops.

Leaving the hotel, a guard ran after me and told me to hide my camera as it wouldn't be safe to go out looking like a tourist. We wondered if we should change hotels but decided against it.

We later found out that the trays belonged to James. In a fit of pique he had ordered a round or two of room service.

Tantalisingly, from our hotel room window we could see the National Art Gallery, but to reach it we had to cross tram lines near the 'necklacing' railway and through Jack Mincer Park, an area rarely entered then by white people. This was 1990, of course, and old habits die hard.

'You can't stay here,' insisted James. 'You must come back to the Cape with me.' By this time he was well and truly settled, really loving his time in South Africa, having made many friends, and was well established in the local rugby scene.

Luckily, we weren't in a position to change our plans as our return flight home, booked from Johannesburg, was in a week's time and we had lots to see. We said our goodbyes to James and shortly after walked across Jack Mincer Park to what proved to be a superb art gallery, introducing me to lovely landscape paintings by J H Pierneef, more of Maggie Laubser and fabulous Anton van Wouw bronzes. In fact, we went several times, finishing each visit in its delightful café, sampling rooibos tea.

Determined to make the most of our stay, we planned sight-seeing trips. These included a gold mine, Heia Safari, as recommended by our fellow traveller on the Blue train, the Voortrekker Monument and Johannesburg Zoo.

The zoo on the city outskirts proved a marvellous experience. Many docile animals and birds were housed in low-fenced enclosures, and none were attempting to get out. They looked pretty content, munching and pecking away with the occasional glance in our direction. We discovered an area with beautiful ancient rock drawings, all positioned exactly as they had been found on the ground in their original locations around South Africa. It was here in the zoo that I saw my only elephant.

Exploring the city, we made our way to busy Bree Street. The atmosphere was so joyous and the street 'choc-a-bloc' with people all the way down to the Market Street Theatre Complex. We progressed slowly, shoulder to shoulder, with thousands of black heads bobbing in the sunshine. Passing stalls with juicy corn cobs roasting, street hairdressers and even a small choir, we eventually arrived at a fabulous market alongside the theatre. We had never experienced anything like it before. It was a heady mix of African artefacts and cultures, with vendors coming from as far away as Zimbabwe and Mozambique to sell their wares. Laid out on the pavements before us were colourful beaded belts, ceremonial aprons and Sangoma dolls, together with thousands of beautifully crafted wooden carvings. I fell in love with a simple carving of a bird with thin steel legs, a long curved beak and a knowing look in its eye. I bought it from its maker called 'Doctor'. I have a photograph of Doctor carving away at a giraffe with, at his feet, 'my bird' peeping out at me from the crowd of carvings!

On a warm autumn day we visited South Africa's administrative capital Pretoria, the Jacaranda City. Here in this beautiful garden city the pace was leisurely compared with the bustle of Johannesburg. We walked along tree-lined avenues and gazed at stately white buildings under a bright blue cloudless sky. Overlooking the city, the Union Buildings offer panoramic views, and we enjoyed ambling through its extensive terraced gardens and parkland. It would be here, in front of massing crowds and televised to the whole world, that Nelson Mandela would be inaugurated as President of the 'rainbow nation' in 1994.

Heeding the recommendation from our fellow traveller on the Blue Train, we booked a 40 kilometre coach trip to Heia Safari and the Mzumba dancers. En route we were taken to George Harrison Park and the site of an old battery mill used to crush ore. This Mr Harrison first discovered gold here, but sadly selling his share just before the massive rush which eventually turned Johannesburg into the Golden City.

Heia Safari truly was an incredible experience. After enjoying a braai lunch and surrounded by zebra, we eventually settled under a thatched stand to watch tribal dances of amazing power and vigour. The energy and skill of the dancers was breathtaking. In the intense afternoon heat even sitting in the shade was uncomfortable, but under that glaring sun the dancers were rhythmically leaping and pounding the ground to the continual beat of drums, beautiful dark skin glistening in the sun. It was a spectacle of unbelievable endurance which lasted several hours, eventually ending with a ceremonial dance by the witch doctor chanting for rain. At that very moment, around four o'clock, the bright sky suddenly darkened, clouds gathered, and large drops of rain began to fall. What power!

The next day, back in Johannesburg, we visited the market again. At around four o'clock we were caught in a violent storm, very similar to the one after the rain dance at Heia Safari. With several others we huddled under shop canopies as people ran though the rain for cover. Many wore black bin liners which seemed most sensible and economical. As quickly as the storm started it stopped and out came the sun, drying the streets almost immediately. We discovered it was normal weather at this time of year! The witch doctor at Heia Safari had excellent timing.

Mum always maintained there were three things she would never do: number one, a Safari, two, go down a mine, and three, take an Alaskan cruise. Having loved the safari we now had the opportunity to visit a gold mine, which, of course, we did! Hard-hatted and ready, we joined fellow explorers in a small cage and proceeded to slowly descend in semi-darkness. It was a cramped affair, and I was just thinking how glad I would be to get to the bottom of the shaft when the cage came to a shuddering halt. We were stuck. Getting hotter by the minute and with murmurs of discontent around me, I was beginning to think I would have a panic attack. I could just about see Mum; her eyes were widening by the second. A second jolt and we were free and continued our descent in the darkness. At the base of the shaft, with exclamations of relief, we poured out of the cage. Led along a dark passage, the sides shored up with wooden planks, we eventually came to an area where we were given a candlelight demonstration of how gold was originally mined. What an arduous occupation! In terrible heat and dust, with danger of collapsing shafts, the workers, bent double, drilled for the precious metal. How little we think of this when we buy our jewellery in the West. Our visit ended with a demonstration of gold being poured into a mould to make a brick-sized ingot. Mum had to admit, despite the interrupted descent, she loved it.

I wasn't really sure whether we should do it or not, but we were offered a trip to Soweto. Driving around a poor area in a coach just to gawp seemed insensitive, but we were persuaded when we realised that it was arranged by Soweto itself. It was a humbling experience. Seeking a better quality of life in South Africa, immigrants pour over the country's borders and make for Soweto, where houses of every type and condition can be found. The very poorest were tin shacks huddled together with their few 'portaloos' and shared water taps, yet spotless washing hung out to dry. Some of the roads were dirt tracks, but there was also great development, with new schools, hospitals and modern roads undergoing construction. We passed through an area resembling Millionaires Row, with substantial, high class residences which wouldn't look out of place in the smartest suburbs of Bristol. It gave me quite a different impression of this growing, energetic area.

Our last stop in Soweto was a small factory, run by an Australian man, for those with learning difficulties. It was a well-organised and peaceful workplace, respectful of its workers who produced beautiful woven goods and basketware. Mindful of luggage limitations on our approaching flight home, we purchased perfectly made woven cream-coloured tray cloths, which we use and enjoy to this day.

Before we left for South Africa, we had arranged to contact expat Joan Waiting who was living in Sandton. A high-class residential suburb, Sandton seemed like another Surrey with its English-style shopping mall and houses to match, but in heat and with extremely high levels of security. It was lovely meeting up with Joan and she took us to her new bungalow, which was almost ready for occupation. It was a beautifully built home and could have been dropped into an English suburb without looking out of place. The only drawback of living in Johannesburg was this frightening level of security. Everywhere we could see barred windows and doors, high fences, barbed wire and locked gates.

Our last weekend in Johannesburg was Easter, so we thought we would go to the local church. However, the streets were empty, and the church was closed. Everyone had gone out of town for the holiday.

'Let's go back to the zoo.' So off we went by taxi.

On arrival, just inside the gates, we were approached by a man in safari shirt and shorts. He introduced himself as a Mr Coetzee, the Director of the zoo. He had seen us on our last visit and was impressed by our return. He offered to show us around and answer any questions. We felt like privileged royal guests. In one of the first enclosures we noticed a deer with a large porcupine spine stuck in its cheek. Concerned, we asked when it would be removed.

Mr Coetzee explained they knew about it, and it would be removed eventually! Each night when all the visitors have gone, animals in the less restrictive enclosures jump out and mix as in the wild. This one deer had bothered a porcupine a little too much, and the embedded spine was the consequence. To teach the deer a lesson, they were leaving it in for the day; then, he assured us, it would definitely be removed, and hopefully the deer would leave the porcupine alone in the future.

We found our Easter celebration at the zoo, for, in one building, day-old chicks were hatching. Before we left, and after thanking kind Mr Coetzee, we had our rooibos tea served by white-gloved waiters at the zoo lakeside cafe. Tomorrow we would be leaving for home.

Waiting in Jan Smuts Airport we decided to have a coffee and a last 'Koeksister' – the sweet, syrupy, twisted doughnut so loved by

South Africans. On the next table an elderly black man was talking to two young white women.

'Don't look round now,' said Mum, 'but I am sure that man is Walter Sississus...' She couldn't quite say it. I looked round and of course it was Walter Sisulu, lawyer and friend of Nelson Mandela, who together had been imprisoned in Robben Island. The young women with him were journalists, interviewing him for a magazine.

We were thrilled to see this eminent man but didn't want to intrude. When the interview was finished and Mr Sisulu walked away, I just had to ask the journalists if it really was him. It was, of course.

'We would have loved to have met him but felt too shy,' we told them. They were sorry and off they went.

However, minutes later, who do we see but Walter Sisulu himself walking across the airport concourse, beaming all over his face and obviously making straight for us.

Those very pleasant young women had gone away to find him and tell him there were two English ladies back at the café who were returning home and would love to meet him.

He embraced us in a warm bear hug, and we told him how much we had loved our stay in his wonderful country. After a few moments conversation together he himself had to leave.

What an honour. We left South Africa on a very high note with enduring and quite marvellous memories. I later received a letter with photos of Mr Sisulu and Nelson Mandela.

James arrived back in the UK the following summer. He had come to love South Africa and in his final letter to me he wrote, 'It is true what they say about the red dust of Africa. It never leaves your veins.' How different from his first missive when he was counting not only the months and days but hours and minutes until his return. However, if we hadn't received that unhappy message, Mum and I would never have experienced for ourselves the wonders of the Rainbow Nation.

It was during that summer Peter Clay and I crossed paths in an art exhibition at the Royal West of England Academy. My life was about to change, and it was then I began to look differently at my photographs and use my camera more and more for future paintings rather than just holiday 'snaps'.

Egypt (1991)

As the boys gradually left the nest for university, 15 Beaconsfield Road became too big for one person, and being an Edwardian house, large bills for maintenance would soon be arriving. I wasn't earning enough for the upkeep, and very sadly decided it was time to leave and find a smaller home. How I loved that house. I soon came to realise a rather funny thing about the area. Not many of my neighbours seem to move out, they just swap houses! It is such a lovely, well established and family-orientated community. Neighbours became friends, and nobody wanted to leave unless they had to. Not wanting to move away, I left 15 Beaconsfield Road for a town house in adjoining Worrall Road. I had watched this house for over a year or so as 'For Sale' signs were put up, then removed and replaced by different agents' boards. I wondered what was wrong, as pebble-dash was applied to part of the first-floor wall and then eventually fell off. I looked at several houses, and was thinking of Clifton Village when Mum said 'it is a long way to go for a cup of coffee'. I realised I needed to stay close by, and so my brother and I arranged a viewing of the sad-looking house. On entering we were very pleasantly surprised. It was light and spacious, although needing a lot of attention. The Beaconsfield Road house had only recently been sold to a young family and so I was free to make an offer. It was accepted, and I moved in during the January of 1991.

The previous summer David had graduated in Agricultural Sciences from Wye College in Kent and proceeded to look for a job.

Initially without success, he decided to take whatever was going on a part-time basis and began an assortment of tractor driving, pea vining and hop picking. We admired his tenacity, and knew it wouldn't be long before the right full-time job came along.

In the meantime, Gran offered him a holiday. David hadn't had a proper break for several years and she wanted him to have a treat. I had always really wanted to see Egypt and knew it would be the sort of place he would love to visit, so I quickly made a telephone call.

'David. How would you like a Nile cruise? Gran's treat.'

His immediate reply, with a sigh, was, 'I'd love it.' He couldn't believe his luck. Only later, and on reflection, did he have some slight misgivings, wondering if he would be travelling up the Nile with a lot of 'oldies'.

However, he didn't let on, and the next time he was home in the spring of 1991 we popped into the Broadmead branch of Thomas Cook. Deliberating over when we should actually go and which way to do it, we eventually decided on 'The Magnificent Nile (Special Offer)', 15th to 28th June. This happened to be the cheapest date at £799 per person from Cairo all the way to Aswan, and with eleven days sailing on the Nile. It would be extremely hot, of course, in fact the hottest time of the year – mad dogs and Englishmen came to mind – but after the first Iraqi war Egypt wasn't a popular holiday destination so luxury trips were going at bargain prices, and especially for those crazy enough to go in midsummer. Payment was made and our instructions and itinerary soon followed. We didn't realise it at the time, but we had hit the jackpot.

The day of our departure for Egypt arrived. As requested, at one o' clock on 15th June we met our tour manager, Bassam El Shamma, and the rest of our small party at the EgyptAir check-in desk at Heathrow. We soon found we were in very capable hands. A young, highly intelligent Egyptian Egyptologist, with an excellent command of English, Bassam was an amusing and informative travel companion. At three o'clock we took off for Cairo. Our exotic adventure had begun.

We arrived at night and were swiftly taken to our hotel, the Cairo Semiramis, where we found a fabulous room awaiting us. David and I had to share quarters but neither of us minded, especially taking in the huge air-conditioned room with its balcony overlooking the Nile and city beyond. As we opened the balcony doors to take in the night scene, a stifling heat engulfed us. The air had a strange hot smell, and in the distance we could see minarets and hear the Muezzin calling followers to prayers. It was a truly different world, and we happily fell asleep to the continual and so typical honking of horns in the streets below.

Ahead of the crowds and before the heat of the day, our first outing was to the wondrous Cairo Museum. On all sides and at every turn, astounding treasures of great age and beauty surrounded us: artefacts from Tutankhamen's tomb, as well as his glorious golden mask, incredible statues of all sizes, ancient jewellery, papyrus paintings and, memorably, a glass case housing a Stele dating from around 3000 BC, five thousand years old and still decipherable! It was quite mind blowing to find such culture from so far back in time. You could spend a week taking it all in, but we had to make do with one morning.

I was very taken with a wooden statue of Ka-Aper, the first reading priest, who lived in Memphis around 2,500 BC. He had such a realistic, modern face and looked so very human. In the museum shop I found a lovely papyrus painting of the Geese of Meidum. Earlier we had been admiring this very wall painting, believed to be the oldest then discovered and representing the unification of Upper and Lower Egypt. I had to buy it for David.

Back in the bus we were gelling as a group and enjoying friendly chatter as we made our way back to the hotel for lunch and a freshen up. We were now quite accustomed to the continual blaring of car horns which accompanied our slow progress.

Our afternoon tour took in the Pyramids and Sphinx at Giza. Like many before, we were surprised to see how close these monuments are to the encroaching city, yet still surrounded by desert. Here our camels awaited. They lay quietly in the sand with their keepers alongside, looking expectantly as we all approached completely covered up against the burning sun and carrying large water bottles. It seemed so bizarre; yesterday a warmish England, and today a boiling hot desert.

'Don't give the men any baksheesh until the ride is over, or they will drop you off too soon,' warned Bassam.

David was first up on the camel. It looked a pretty precarious operation, but when my turn came I smiled bravely and tightly held a slippery leather knob on its saddle for dear life as the animal heaved itself up, rocking forwards and back with some violence I have to say. Off we trotted, water bottle thumping against my side with each lanky step.

To my horror, David's camel started to gallop, his keeper running alongside. 'Oh, please no!' I thought. 'I really don't want to do that. I'll fall off'. Thankfully my little keeper, continually talking I know not what, but probably asking for baksheesh, kept on walking, and it was only after the strenuous dismounting process that David told me he had asked to make the camel run. Evidently a bone-rattling experience, and one I was quite happy to forego.

Arriving at the largest pyramid of Cheops, shiny and sticky with heat, we were led along a cramped and stifling tunnel to an inner chamber. It was a claustrophobic experience, dark, hot and uncomfortable as we crouched down to fit through, but we weren't going to miss anything. To think we were actually inside a pyramid! Eventually we were very glad to get out, with my pulse racing due to the stifling atmosphere.

In bright sunshine the air was full of dust and a pungent camel smell, but exciting nonetheless. We walked over to the Great Sphinx, now a shadow of its former self, having been eroded over time by sand and rendered noseless by the Mamalukes' cannon shot. In previous centuries, it had been used as target practice! Finally, we were ushered into an air-conditioned building housing an ancient and obviously very precious boat, largely intact, before returning to the city. Tomorrow we would be starting our Nile cruise.

After our early morning call and breakfast in the hotel, we boarded the coach and attempted an exit onto the main road. There was the usual traffic chaos and horns continually blaring, so we expected a difficult and extended ride to the boat. As if by magic the horn honking stopped as people poured out of their cars and proceeded to direct the traffic, allowing us out. It was unexpectedly charming.

Arriving at the waterfront and the *Royal Orchid*, our home for the next eleven days, we admired her compact, sleek lines. We were the only group on board and soon settled in, slipping easily into the cruising lifestyle. As before, David and I shared a cabin but it was spacious and comfortable, with a large picture window overlooking the Nile. We didn't give it another thought. By that time David had palled up with a delightful group of young people and spent most of his time with them. These were Rachael and Alex, two recently qualified teachers, Simon, a bank clerk, and a young married lady from Scotland whose name I have now forgotten. It was only later, meeting for lunch, when another couple came over to introduce themselves and we realised there had been some confusion.

'Have you and your husband visited Egypt before?' they asked.

Oh dear. Poor David! We quickly explained we were sharing for economic reasons only. Kind as ever, David let it pass without comment, his face showing some dismay, but he soon disappeared to join his new young friends.

Sailing out of Cairo, we swooshed through swathes of blue-flowered water hyacinth and excitedly anticipated the next ten days. Bassam was proving to be a wonderfully funny and knowledgeable companion who had the ability to make Egyptian history really live. We knew we were in for a treat.

On the upper deck I watched the land slipping by. It was fascinating. However, I was taken aback to see two older couples intensely swapping stories of grandchildren as, quite unnoticed by them, scenery of truly biblical proportions passed them by. I retreated to the lower deck.

As we settled into little like-minded groups, it soon became apparent that there was the upper bar and pool deck type of passenger, and those who preferred the quieter lower deck for reading and taking in the scenery. I still needed plenty of rest and enjoyed the quiet companionship down below. The boat had extensive canopies on both decks, and there were comfortable wooden loungers for all. The only time I saw David was when, as the sun and boat changed direction, he arrived to drag my heavy lounger back into the shade. The decks eventually became so hot it was impossible to go barefoot. I had never experienced dry burning heat like this, and as I watched Egyptian rural life on the river banks, it dawned on me that there was no canopy and lounger for the people who had to live and work in these extreme conditions.

We passed typical Nile villages with their boxy white buildings and well-loaded donkeys trotting under date palms. Running as fast as they could, children waved, excitedly calling to us as white-sailed feluccas and overloaded small boats silently passed. In the fertile land either side of the river, men would momentarily cease their toil and, leaning on their spades, watch us sail by. Their life and dress would not have changed in thousands of years.

Our first stop was Beni Hasan and the hillside tombs. Disembarking, we passed some of the crew who were making the most of a little time off smoking their gurgling waterpipes and smiling as we passed by. It was a steep climb up to the tombs, but we relished the thought of being some of the few tourists to see them. Most

Nile cruises are taken from Luxor to Aswan, and not many ply the whole navigable river from Cairo to Aswan.

Sitting outside the tombs, the view was spectacular: over the fertile land to the river where we were one of three boats moored. We later learned that these three vessels were the only tourist boats currently operating on the Nile. The rest were moored side by side at Luxor, empty and forlorn.

It was fairly dark inside the tombs, but we earnestly studied the hieroglyphics, all made so interesting by Bassam. Suddenly, a cracking sound made us all jump. David, in the gloom, had trodden on a floor-level light casing. The caretaker, white robes flowing and a cross look on his face, approached, clicking his fingers for baksheesh. At that very moment, an elderly lady in our party, Jane, appeared to be intently scrutinising the tomb walls, leaning closer and closer, until she keeled over. She had fainted. With military precision, and with the spotlight now off David, the caretaker and his assistant carried the patient out into the fresh air and proceeded to waft her with their long white robes. Out of their pockets came slices of lemon which they pressed to her lips. I wondered how hygienic that was, but it seemed to do the trick. The dear lady came round and, as she opened her eyes, blinking in the sunlight, the two men were clicking their fingers again, this time asking her for baksheesh. Naturally, at that moment she wouldn't have known what was happening, so I paid the tip. It seemed only fair as David had cracked the light casing.

The eleven days passed in a marvellous whirl of temples, tombs, biblical landscapes and anxious vendors. It could be intimidating being pressed on all sides by village men and women desperate to sell anything, just short of actually giving their wares away. It was a sad and desperate time for them, but we couldn't buy everything. I soon learned never to make eye contact if I wasn't interested in the wares on offer. This was made easier by wearing sunglasses and moving swiftly on, saying a loud, 'La shokran' – 'No thank you!'

On the fifth day after Beni Hasan we visited the ruined Temple of Thoth, the Baboon God, at Ashmounein, also known as the Greek Hermopolis. Here we found a huge statue of a baboon just sitting by the roadside. Later I glimpsed a little girl working a shadouf, an ancient water pump, as we travelled on by coach to the necropolis at Tuna el-Gebel. By now the midday sun was so intense we were desperate to find some shade. There was very little, and the site of a large group of people making for a small patch of shade must have looked very amusing. The strength of the June rays, compounded by very little shade and yet even more heat reflected up from the desert floor, made for an uncomfortable visit, but I have to say I am glad to have experienced it. Here in the middle of the desert we absorbed the unusual mix of Egyptian and Hellenic wall paintings.

Back at the boat, and a welcome opportunity to cool down, we enjoyed afternoon tea served by white-gloved waiters. We looked at the noticeboard in the foyer to see what was on offer for dinner that night. The staff were hand-picked and highly trained but, as so often with different cultures, there are opportunities for hilarious language mistakes. On the noticeboard, the pudding that evening was described as *'Strawberry Fartelets'*. We laughed all week.

The next morning David felt a little 'off colour', hopefully not because of the strawberry 'fartelets', and decided against the trip that day, a tractor ride deep into the desert. It was such a shame he missed this experience.

As we travelled into the desert, bumping slowly along in the shaded trailers, children from a remote village happily ran with us, their brown legs flying. We eventually reached the archaeological site of el-Amarna, the Pharaoh Akhenaton's short-lived capital, dedicated to the sun god Aton. There were three marvellous tombs. One belonged to poor Akhenaton, he of the strange egg-shaped head, as was his beautiful wife-sister Nefertiti, probably the result of a line of incestuous marriages.

The *Royal Orchid* was moored at a riverside village. On our return the children excitedly pressed forward to sell baskets they had made. A village elder, armed with a rifle, shouted at them to behave. He sounded and looked rather terrifying, bearded and dressed in dark robes. It was a typical village scene, with people collecting water, washing dishes and clothes as water buffalo placidly drank, their legs submerged to cool down.

I bought some baskets and decided to give one to Auntie Gwen back in Kingswood. She loved children so much but was never able to have her own.

We passed many of these villages as we made our way to Luxor and there seemed to be a riverside etiquette. Animals in first, followed above them by clothes washing, dish washing, then a little further on water was taken for cooking and drinking. However, the next village just a little further upstream was doing the same thing.

On 21st June we had a day of leisurely sailing. I bought a turquoise galabeya from the on-board shop in readiness for a party planned by the staff that evening. After dinner I went to bed, but soon after settling down to read David arrived. 'You must come and look at this, Mum!' We were sailing along in the dark, and on the river bank were a series of fires; a result of a 'hot storm' up from India, said Bassam.

As the cruise got underway I had befriended a like-minded married couple, Chris and Trish, who had met working on P&O liners, he as First Officer and she as a nanny. Chris had only just taken command of a British Telecom cable laying boat, and both were somewhat discriminating where cruises were concerned. However, they memorably declared, 'This holiday started as wonderful ... and just gets better.'

The next day, June 22nd, the day before my birthday, we arrived at Abydos where we were surprised to find a Thomas Cook coach, adorned with Arabic writing, waiting to transport us to the famous temple.

In bright sunlight we climbed steep steps to the courtyard and then, over chunks of rocks and boulders, the temple appeared. This plain fronted, multi-pillared building could not prepare us for the treasures inside. It was here for us that Bassam brought to life beautiful wall paintings and reliefs. Most memorable was that of a horned bull with ribs visible through its flesh. Bassam explained how the sculptor had brilliantly caught the animal in mid-breath. His enthusiasm was infectious and we, absolutely riveted by his colourful descriptions, couldn't wait for more.

One corridor housed the Tablet of Abydos, which recorded the names of seventy-six rulers of Egypt. Inside the hall of huge columns it was hot and gloomy, and we sat in the dust around the column bases to drink water, recompose ourselves and digest all these facts. In such heat it was difficult to stand for long periods, and sitting on a grubby ledge was the last thing I would normally do; but, along with the others, I was so grateful for any chance to rest. It took me by surprise when perspiration poured down my back as if a tap had been turned on. I decided to put some salt and honey on my breakfast rolls each morning, and keep drinking! It seemed to do the trick.

Back to the boat for lunch, and then on to the Graeco-Roman temple of Dendera, one of the best-preserved temple complexes in Egypt and dedicated to Hathor, goddess of love and joy.

Arriving back at the boat, villagers were waiting for us; the children selling their homemade woollen fans, and adults with piles of brightly coloured shish (stoles). We all bought something before boarding the boat. Waving goodbye to the happy crowd below, we set sail, thinking about the next day's adventure – the Valleys of the Kings and Queens at Thebes.

The day of my birthday dawned brightly, and although I had kept quiet about it, David obviously hadn't. Cards arrived from fellow passengers, and Bassam announced there would be a party that evening! But first we had another wonderful day visiting the traditional burial grounds of the pharaohs and their queens on the west bank of the Nile. Our coach transported us through palm trees and sugar plantations, into the arid desert and stillness of the Valleys of the Kings and Queens. We wandered around, enjoying the magnificence of the tombs of Seti I, Queen Hapshetsut and Ramesses III. We were bowled over by it all. To think that in a few years' time, this peace, in surroundings of such splendour, would be cruelly interrupted by gunmen. Those tourists, like us that day, would have been quietly milling around, unaware of the horrors awaiting them. Indeed, our very hotel in Cairo, the Semi-Ramis, would suffer the same fate. It brings home how trusting and innocent we are when on holiday in foreign lands. In 1991 we were lucky to find nothing but kindness and courtesy.

Driving back to *Royal Orchid* we came across the famous Colossi of Memnon, two gigantic statues standing alone in the desert. It is said that each sunrise a prolonged sound or song is emitted by the most southerly of the monuments. Sadly, not being sunrise, we couldn't confirm it, but we enjoyed standing like dots under their immensity.

That night, it was party time – Egyptian style! We all dressed up in our new galabeyas and various styles of head gear, some looking distinctly uncomfortable but bravely carrying it off. After dinner, chatting amongst ourselves, we were startled by loud singing and a great clashing of cymbals. Led by Bassam, the appropriately dressed crew arrived singing and beating cymbals as they processed towards us bearing cake. A tray displaying a huge confection complete with candles was duly presented. My birthday cake! The crew were intent on a good party! I felt really embarrassed with all this attention focused on me, but also quite moved. It was such a happy occasion for passengers and the crew, everyone smiling and laughing, with movie cameras zooming in and photographers clicking away. This must be what it is like for the famous as paparazzi home in. I was being treated like a celebrity by people who barely knew me. It was a wonderful evening, and we finished dancing to the music in best Egyptian manner.

The town of Luxor was next, and soon after mooring alongside the Corniche I joined David's cheerful young band in a horse driven caleche, making for designer shops and Benetton t-shirts. That night there was an optional excursion to the Temples of Karnak for the 'Sound and Light' performance, but I decided to give it a miss as it was all in French that night. I was looking forward to the next day when we would be seeing Karnak and Luxor in all its sunlit splendour.

It is hard to believe, but with a photograph to prove it, I am staring up at one of the massive columns in the famous Hall of Columns with not another soul to be seen. I have never forgotten how quiet it was, and how dwarfed I was by these huge structures.

We had another magnificent, hot, blue sky day of temples, statues, obelisks and sphinxes. By this time we couldn't get enough of Bassam's talks on Egypt's fascinating history, laced with exotic names - Queen Hatshepsut, Ramesses, Amenophis, the sun god Amun-Ra, his wife Mut, and their son, the moon god Khonsu. At a small booth by the Sacred Lake, I purchased yet another film; there was so much to record. I have to admit to spending a lot of time on my own taking photographs, leaving David with Bassam in the small escorted group, knowing he would fill me in with all the historical details later. I just couldn't miss any photo opportunities.

That night we sailed for the colourful Nile town of Esna. Here was another impressive temple, dedicated to the ram god Khnum, but first we had to navigate the little town and its main shopping street. Less of a shopping street, and more of a higgledy-piggledy row of sun-sheltered booths, all manned by eager vendors of treasures hidden within. The shopkeepers called and beckoned us over. With my background, and never one to resist a shop, I approached an interesting booth with a kindly-faced owner. I picked up a beautifully crocheted white prayer cap and asked the price. The starting price was a bit of a try-on, but after good-natured bargaining, the cap was mine. We both laughed as the bargaining was fun and fair, for him as well.

As I turned away to catch up with the group, he said, 'You must give me a present.' Suddenly, Bassam appeared at my side. 'You should give her a present. It's her birthday.'

The man immediately smiled broadly and disappeared into the booth, returning with a lovely blue scarab bead. He bowed and gave it to me with obvious pleasure, not wanting to take anything for it. I felt quite overwhelmed, and after thanking him for such a treasure Bassam and I returned to the group. This delightful incident was typical of the good-natured Egyptians we met in 1991. I have the bead to this day, carefully attached to one of my lace bobbins.

June 25th brought us to Edfu, where horse-drawn carriages transported us to the temple of the falcon-headed god Horus. I found this monumental temple with its great pylons particularly fascinating. Building commenced by King Ptolemy, it took 180 years to complete and contains scenes depicting the might and glory of the pharaohs. Sunlight was most effectively reflected into its very dark interior by white robed men holding cardboard flags covered with tin. Leaving Edfu, I purchased a most skilfully carved small stone statue of Horus.

On returning to the boat, we set sail for the temple of Kom Ombo, Bassam's favourite. Beautifully situated overlooking the Nile, this temple is dedicated to both Sobek, the crocodile god, and Horus, so as not to offend either. The figures represented here are more rounded and human looking than the typically slender forms we had seen previously. Here we posed for a group photo. It is an honest record of a very happy and relaxed party.

During afternoon tea we set sail for Aswan and had a welcome early night. The next day we were to make an early flight 340 km south to Abu Simbel near the Sudan border, and it was important to get there before the intense heat of the day made it unbearable.

Abu Simbel is the finest and largest monument in Nubia, built by Ramesses II to commemorate his victory over the Hittites in Syria. Hewn out of stone, and with four mighty statues, this tremendous monument, with its smaller temple alongside dedicated to Ramesses's wife Nefertari, was moved block by block between 1965 and 1972; a huge and impressive undertaking to rescue it from the encroaching Nile waters with the building of the great Aswan Dam. This masterpiece, reinforced by resin and steel braces, now lies in safety 90 metres above its original site.

Our afternoon treat on returning to Aswan was a relaxing sail on board the silent white sailed feluccas to the lush gardens of Kitchener's Island, and then on to view the Aga Khan's resting place. Sailing past the Old Cataract Hotel, from where Agatha Christie wrote 'Death on the Nile', we decided to pay a visit that evening. It was a delightfully peaceful and perfect interlude after another full day. As we came back alongside the riverbank, Nubian women were waiting. They looked a little suspicious, probably because we couldn't help looking at them and admiring their obvious beauty. A few smiles were eventually exchanged.

Our wonderful holiday would soon be at an end, and this was brought home when we arrived back at the boat to find instructions to leave our luggage outside our cabins by 7.45 the next morning. We were all going to have to say goodbye to *Royal Orchid* and each other. But first, there was, of course, an excellent excuse for another party.

Our farewell party was a colourful, noisy affair, and even the 'Gong Boy' in his red fez joined in the dancing. Another large cake arrived and we all proceeded to tuck in. To finish off the evening, a few of us decided this would have to be the time to visit the Old Cataract Hotel. We piled into a waiting caleche and made our way up. Our journey was a sobering one as the poor horse was lame, so we got off and paid the man a bit extra to get his animal attended to. The sad creature could hardly walk, and the man kept urging him on. He promised he would get help, but probably didn't.

I have never forgotten this sad beast, and all the others working so hard in the heat of an Egyptian summer. A few years later, when an opportunity came to subscribe to the Brooke Clinic, who treat such working animals and attempt to ease their burden, I did so without a moment's hesitation.

After an hour or so enjoying the genteel delights of the famous old hotel, we walked back to the boat.

Thursday 27th June dawned, and with our luggage outside as requested, off we all went for a little more sightseeing en route to the airport. We walked around a large unfinished obelisk, then to the dams; first the Old Dam, and then the two-mile-long High Dam, said to be the largest rock-filled dam in the world. A boat ride took us to a sacred island dedicated to the god Isis and our final temple, that of Philae and its graceful kiosk. The remains of the original edifice are still visible, built around 300 years BC by the last native King of Egypt, King Nectanebus. The other two temples here date, as do Dendera and Edfu, from the late Ptolemaic period. There was a tradition that every Egyptian should make at least one pilgrimage to the island as it was believed that the miraculous and beneficial flooding of the Nile originated here. The richly fertile, well-tended banks we had sailed by over the last ten days were a testament to this.

To save these temples from the advancing Nile, the site was moved brick by brick 150 metres north, following the construction of the Old Dam at the beginning of the 20th century.

By lunchtime we were at Aswan Airport for our flight back to Cairo. One more night at the Semiramis, then our sad goodbyes to Bassam at Cairo airport and our flight to London.

Mum came up to Heathrow to meet us, wanting to find out first-hand how good the holiday had been. 'Someone's had a great time,' she called as a berry-brown David with an obvious bounce in his step appeared through the arrivals gate. They hugged each other.

'Thanks, Gran!'

It was a definite turning point for David, who arrived home to an excellent permanent job offer. I happily relived it all, filling several photo albums, and often still say, 'Wasn't our Egyptian holiday wonderful, David?'

Soon after we returned, I worked on a pastel picture of the Nile. For the first time, I was using a selection of my photos for this work to capture the essence of Egypt.

The Highland and Islands of Scotland (1992)

After seeing a gorgeous newspaper photo of a light and watery Benbecula, I wanted to experience the Outer Hebrides for myself.

Weather conditions permit summer visits only, so when we saw this very trip advertised as a coach tour with Wallace Arnold for June of 1992, Mum and I decided to book up straight away. We had always loved our many visits to Scotland, especially all the family holidays from Northumberland, but up to that point the furthest north we had ventured was Inverness.

We met up with our coach party at Gordano, the M5 Service Station on the outskirts of Bristol. Suitcases aboard and settling in comfortably, we set off for Carlisle, our first stop. Here, on the outskirts of town, we were herded into a rather bleak hotel. I started to have misgivings. Dinner was served in a canteen-style dining room, and I found myself sitting next to a man with very scabby arms. I was beginning to think this was a terrible mistake.

After dinner I took myself off for a walk around the rather dull local area, seriously considering packing it in and going straight home. Poor Mum. Calling me a bit of a snob, she eventually persuaded me to stay. It could possibly and hopefully improve, so I grudgingly gave in and thought I'd better give it another day or two. Mum visibly relaxed. It seems rather dramatic now, but I had such high expectations of beauty and fun. Typical of my unrealistic view of life, I thought. Irresponsibly optimistic as usual.

The next day we set off for Scotland and our hotel in the Highlands. Stopping off at the delightful town of Moffat and then the Salmon Leap at Pitlochry, I had to admit things were improving... but only slightly. Mum was beginning to relax and happily chatted with fellow passengers, A visit to the Scottish Wool shop raised her spirits even further.

Our hotel was beautifully situated in the Highlands at Strathpeffer near Dingwall, but unfortunately the food was only marginally better than Carlisle! We were experiencing old-fashioned coach-trip catering. A visit to the Museum of Childhood lifted spirits. Here we found really charming old photographs, including a quite telling one from the 19th century of a poor highland boy aged about nine – no socks or shoes and wearing a heavily patched kilt, but clutching in one hand a freshly caught salmon. His other hand shaded his eyes against bright sunlight as he looked directly into the camera lens. His name was Donald MacDonald, and he looked in need of a big hug.

Straight after breakfast the following day, our first stop was a wine tour of Lord Lovat's Estate in the Fraser stronghold of Moniack Castle. It was about 10am and the tastings were generous, but luckily we were also offered biscuits with jam made on the estate. We piled back into the coach, our purchases clinking away. I nursed a bottle of Silver Birch Wine for Robert. He was soon to graduate in Performance Arts from Middlesex University, and his middle name is Fraser!

The coach immediately made for the Muir of Ord and the Ord Distillery and by 11 o'clock we were on a tour, followed by 'The Tastings'. I'm not a great imbiber of the strong stuff, but Glen Ord single malt was quite something. We were handed large glassfuls of the golden liquid which slipped easily down in all its silkiness, and second helpings were not refused. From then on, we were all the greatest of pals!

I don't remember lunch that day.

What I do remember is a brief stop at the Glen Docherty gift shop, more of a cabin at the side of a lay-by. We piled out of the coach, not to visit the shop but to stand at the roadside with our binoculars to await a sighting of golden eagles, We were not disappointed, and soon a majestic bird glided into view. Mum's face was a mix of great surprise and delight.

Before reaching Ullapool and the Caledonian MacBrayne ferry to Stornoway, we enjoyed a tranquil walk around the lovely Gardens of Inverewe. The sun was shining in Ullapool as we sailed away from the quayside and the sea looked quite calm, but as we ventured into deeper waters the boat started rocking and swaying. It was obviously an older boat, with very little in the stabilisation department. Never a good traveller, this was not a pleasant voyage for me or for many of our party. In fact, it was an absolute nightmare, and best skimmed over!

After a brief but welcome pause to offload some passengers on Skye, we eventually arrived in a grey but attractive Stornoway, the capital of Lewis. With great relief, we disembarked and gradually stopped swaying from side to side as we found our land legs, and proceeded to enjoy a good walk around this peaceful and friendly town. Before island hopping our way south, we needed to visit a bank. Joining the queue, we waited our turn. When we arrived at the counter, the young clerk in her lovely sing-song accent started to ask us where we came from and where we were going... in great depth. I looked nervously round at the rest of the queue, only to find smiling faces from similarly interested folk. Not an impatient look to be seen. We were definitely in foreign parts! It was delightful.

On Lewis we visited an ancient blackhouse with an aromatic peat fire burning, and then moved on to the mysterious standing stones of Callanish. Passing curved lines of freshly cut peat, the stones mystically appeared on the horizon, their grey, gnarled fingers pointing to the sky.

On this bleak and windy hillside, we walked in and around the incredible circle and avenues, learning some of its history. It was an eerie and magical experience, especially hearing of the remnants of human bones found in a multi-chambered tomb. Constructed approximately 5,000 years ago by prehistoric tribesmen from southern Europe, it is believed these structures bore a distinct relation to heavenly patterns. Over the years, some of the 54 stones fell down and were eventually covered in almost two metres of peat. In 1857 the former owner of Lewis, Sir James Matheson, removed the peat and restored the site to its present magnificence.

Next stop was, of course, the unmissable Harris Tweed factory. A small building, it seemed literally to be a cottage industry. Genuine Harris Tweed must be made from one hundred per cent pure virgin Scottish wool, dyed, spun and finished in the Outer Hebrides, and then hand woven by the islanders in their homes. Only genuine Harris Tweed is stamped with the certification mark, or Orb Mark as it is known.

We were entertained to lunch in the village hall, prepared by really sweet local women, and here we could buy small Harris Tweed items. I immediately spied a plump tea cosy and quickly bought it before settling down to lunch. I still use and treasure this lovely item, now with a heavily tea-stained lining, but the Orb Mark still proudly visible.

Making our way to the harbour for our hop to North Uist, we had a few moments to visit the Harris Tweed Shop. This was the size of a small garage, crammed with tweed and with a comforting woolly smell. Using poor Mum for sizing again, we found flat caps made with various tweed offcuts for the boys. Eventually locating three good fits, they were bagged up just in time for us to catch the ferry. Mum hurriedly combed her hair before boarding.

Thankfully it was a short and more stable voyage heading to North Uist, where we disembarked and travelled south through bleak but strangely beautiful, watery countryside to Benbecula.

Arriving in Tigharry, I noticed how sparse the gardens were. The low white houses, built to withstand powerful elements, all had small gardens with washing flying briskly on their lines, but very few plants. Delicate flowers could not possibly survive here. I walked on alone to an empty white sandy beach where a huge wind turbine stood sentinel. Eerily rotating and humming away on its massive steel skeleton, it was an impressive and rather magnificent lone structure.

Driving on through South Uist, we boarded the next ferry to beautiful Barra. On board, alongside our coach stood a huge lorry covered in seaweed. 'Lobsters', we were told, 'Making their way to France.' Well I never! I wonder how often we had tucked into fish when boating in France and thinking it was all local.

Landing in Castlebay, we soon realised we must be in one of the most lovely places on the Outer Hebrides. Gaelic was softly spoken in the main street, and fishermen's cottages, small boats and lobster pots lined the long white curved bay overlooking the water to Kisimul Castle, the stronghold of the MacNeils of Barra. We knew we would enjoy our stay here. Our hotel was situated on another bay a short drive away. Accompanied by the calls of oystercatchers and very white sheep, we found ourselves walking along the bay in soft daylight at 11 o'clock at night.

The next morning we decided to visit the castle, and found a willing ferryman, Donald Patrick Sinclair. This delightfully ruddy-faced, elderly gentleman in his yellow oilskins and peaked sailor cap entertained us with a commentary as he rowed over to the small island and castle. A quietly spoken Hebridean, he told us of his father, Murdo Sinclair, the first Barra Lifeboat Coxswain. As I looked at his wonderful face, I asked if I could photograph him. There was no problem. He was quite used to it, having been the subject of famous photographers in the past. I felt in illustrious company and wondered to myself whether I might work on a portrait of him on my return home. Here, on Barra, there was a wealth of material for landscapes, as well as this great face and lovely personality.

Kisimul Castle on its tiny island is easily explored in an hour or so. From its roof, admiring an old signalling beacon and enjoying the tremendous view, we saw Donald arrive back, calling to us. During the short return to Castlebay, Donald told us of the time he had, by mistake, left some visitors behind. It was so lovely, listening to him talk in his gentle voice with the water lapping the side of the boat. I have never forgotten the story.

This one day, as normal, he made his final return to the castle and called out for the last time to make sure everyone knew he was about to go home. The few remaining visitors clambered into the rowing boat and off they went, Donald anticipating supper back in his cottage by the shore.

Some time later, with Donald enjoying his meal by the fireside, there came a knock at the door. It was an anxious neighbour with news that two people had been left on the island. He looked out to see them waving from the castle ramparts. Making a hasty return, he found a very relieved young American couple. They apologised for not hearing his earlier call: 'We were by the "trash can" on the roof.'

This was the beacon! Donald quietly chuckled as he remembered it.

The next day we visited the little local airport with its famous airstrip on the long sands, and watched small, two-engined, Loganair planes landing and taking off with their handful of passengers.

The air was so fresh and clean. We all felt quite rejuvenated, but rather sad as we knew we would soon be returning to the mainland. Before that, however, we visited a small and very peaceful hillside graveyard overlooking the sea. Here we searched for the last resting place of a famous Hebridean, the author Sir Compton MacKenzie of 'Whisky Galore' fame.

'I've found it!' called out a proud Mum. She was the first to spot it. It made her day.

All too soon we were on the ferry to Oban, but this time the trip was smooth as silk. Thankfully this was a more up-to-date vessel with good stabilisers. After passing Tobermory on the island of Mull, we eventually arrived in Oban and were back on the coach for our last stop, Glasgow.

We arrived at the Stakis Hotel in the centre of Glasgow to a most wonderful welcome as honoured guests. Ooh, the breakfasts! Porridge with cream, kippers and smoked salmon. Our last few days in Scotland were so good. Mum and I decided to take the bus to the Burrell Collection at Pollok Park.

This impressive museum, built especially for the Burrell Collection in 1972, but now recently updated and enlarged, houses international objects and art of the most superb kind, reflecting the taste of its benefactor, Sir William Burrell. He and his wife donated the collection, together with money to house it, to the City of Glasgow in 1944. Such is the size of this completely wonderful collection that not all of it can be displayed at the same time. Each piece exhibited, whether architectural, pottery, fabric, furniture or art, is absolutely choice, and it was here that I found and fell in love with the work of Joseph Crawhall. Born in 1861, a Tynesider and one of the 'Glasgow Boys', Joseph Crawhall produced the most exquisite paintings in pastel, oils and watercolours. His studies of animals and birds, together with farming and hunting scenes, are as fresh and lively as if produced only yesterday. They are a delight to behold, and an inspiration to any artist. I never cease to enjoy dipping into the book of his work, purchased that day at the Burrell. In the book I found his famous painting 'The Aviary in Clifton Zoo', a lively row of parrots on stands.

The morning we left Glasgow, our waitresses came on board the coach to sing Scottish songs and wave farewell. What hospitality!

One more stop to go, and as before we were herded into an impersonal hotel somewhere in England. What a disappointing finale. Apart from the rumpus I caused by asking for an apple instead of the pudding presented at dinner, a plastic looking sponge, everything else there has thankfully been erased. Luckily all the marvellous memories of our previous two weeks made that blot on the itinerary as nothing.

Thank goodness I stayed with this trip after the disappointing start in Carlisle. There must be a lesson in it somewhere for me!

Vietnam (1993)

Once more, an article and photograph in a newspaper travel supplement led to the next adventure.

As I turned the page, a photograph leapt out. Incredible rocky outcrops pointed skywards, with fishermen in junks sailing on a limpid sea. It was a breathtakingly beautiful scene, and one I wanted to see for myself. Reading on, I found this to be Vietnam and the magical Ha Long Bay, formed, it is said, by the thrashings of a dragon's tail. Never dreaming I would ever get there, I showed Mum the photo and forgot all about it.

The following spring, Mum toddled up Beaconsfield Road with the RSPB magazine she had just received. In it was advertised 'Bird Trip to Vietnam with Tony Soper', and with a departure date that very September. This was more of an expedition cruise which included the whole length of Vietnam, sailing from Hong Kong to the Chinese island of Hainan by way of the Gulf of Tonkin and South China Sea, eventually finishing at Fraser's Hill in Malaysia.

'I'll pay!' offered Mum.

'Ooh. Yes please.' This was too good an opportunity for any second thoughts, and the booking was promptly made. It was only a little later I started having a few doubts. It had been advertised as the first group to enter Vietnam since the war with America in the 1960s. Fairly hefty anti-malarial medication would be needed. What if we didn't come back? I said nothing of this to Mum as she was so thrilled and excited to have found this trip. I suppressed any doubts, and off we went.

The departure day arrived and we made our way to Heathrow and a BA flight to Hong Kong. On the plane we settled in comfortably next to a businessman from Hong Kong, a kind and pleasant man. The journey went well until Mum, disorientated by the time changes, took her blood pressure pills at the wrong time and felt faint and ill. Summoning the hostess, I asked if there was anywhere Mum could lie down. I was horrified by her negative response and lack of attention. No, there wasn't, and no assistance was offered.

Our neighbour suggested removing the armrests so Mum could lie down on our two seats and lean against him. This we did, and I perched on the outer arm rest for hours until poor Mum eventually recovered. It certainly put us off using BA in the future.

Arriving in a hot, sticky and crowded Hong Kong, our troubles behind us, we were transported to the very smart Hilton Hotel for a three-day stay. Here we met up with the rest of our party and our guide, Tony Soper, who outlined the next few days' activities. However, we were soon stopped in our tracks by Hurricane Becky. Before we had any time to explore the delights of this bustling city, Hong Kong was completely shut down. The planned visit to Lantau Island and our lunch at the monastery was cancelled. We were all locked into the hotel, watching in amazement as street furniture flew by and trees bent double in the grey, lashing ferocity of the storm. Towels had been stuffed against outer doors, and all we could do was sit it out, albeit in comfort. The upmarket hotel shops provided some relief, and we enjoyed a prolonged visit to one superior gift shop where Mum found a really charming Chinese doll for little Emily, my brother John's first child.

By the following day, Becky had veered away and we were able to make our next scheduled trip to the Mai Po Marshes, but the heavily humid heat was overpowering. Mum declared grumpily: 'I can't spend the next three weeks like this in stuffy hides!' She was too heavily dressed in protective clothing against heat and mosquitoes, with socks rolled up over her trousers, a wide-brimmed hat, sunglasses, and only part of her face and hands to be seen. Oh dear. I wondered if we had made the right choice of holiday.

As it turned out there were very few birds to see, apart from a White Throated Kingfisher way in the distance across a lagoon. We felt 'twitching' in tropical climes was not for us, and especially as it seemed to be out of season. Dear Tony did his very best to keep us entertained, especially as we had some very serious, expert birdwatchers in our group, all with professional cameras, tripods and binoculars at the ready.

'Never mind,' I told Mum. 'Although I love birds, we are here more for the culture. Things will improve, I am sure.' There was a sort of 'Hmm' in response.

We found ourselves part of a pleasant group and soon began to enjoy each other's company as we mastered the art of eating dim sum with chopsticks. My first attempt was greeted by laughing from the waiter as he ran over to help me out. The peg-like article I was spearing my dim sum with was a pair of chopsticks, and had to be snapped apart before being used. We soon became experts.

The food was delicious and we loved Hong Kong, although there was not much time left to explore as we were to join our boat, *Caledonian Star*, the following day. With just enough time left to visit the markets and ride the *Star* ferry, we also managed to meet up with some Clifton neighbours, the Pendleton family, who were living in Hong Kong at the time. It seemed very strange and out of context having tea with them there in the Hilton, but it was lovely catching up with their news. I believe the rather superior and very fashionable Hilton has now been demolished and replaced by another high-rise building.

Embarkation day arrived and we were driven to the docks and *Caledonian Star*, our home for the next couple of weeks. That night we left a spectacularly illuminated Hong Kong and made for our first stop, the large Chinese island of Hainan.

In Hong Kong we had been joined by a young English lady with her Hong Kong boyfriend. The girl, who I should call 'Miss J', was obviously disabled but wealthy. She informed us they were to marry and go to Canada, but having only just arrived from the UK the young girl hadn't even met the man's family. Alarm bells rang. When the young man left the ship just before we sailed, poor Tony had the responsibility of keeping his eye on 'Miss J', who kept threatening to leave the group to find her 'boyfriend'.

Things settled a little, and the day at sea provided a relaxing break and an opportunity to get to know our small group of fellow passengers and the friendly crew. Tom Schornak, an American ex-Vietnam veteran, gave an excellent briefing on the itinerary from his point of view, and a most moving account of his wartime experiences. It was then we decided we belonged to Tom's cultural group and to forget about intensive birdwatching, if there was to be any. This eventually proved to be a very sensible decision!

During the voyage that day the cry went out - a bird had been spotted. Only one bird, not even a flock, but I shall never forget the reaction of two of our party. Obviously serious 'twitchers', and laden with large equipment, they set off at quite a pace from the bows to the stern where the lone sighting was believed to be. Trying to keep a straight face, I watched as they both ran through an archway together, and then stuck fast! They freed themselves like corks popping out of a bottle and continued their sprint. At the stern, there was Tony, holding an exhausted reed warbler, a brown, insignificant bird which had just landed on the deck. The poor thing had expired by the next morning. Such enthusiasm for a plain solitary bird. I thought. Without high expectations, I hoped they would not have further disappointments.

A delightful Filipino, the smiling Willie, was our waiter on that first day, and by the next morning we realised we belonged to him. Arriving at breakfast and just considering where we might sit, who should we see but Willie, standing next to a chair with a napkin draped over it, and on the table an identical yoghurt to the one I had requested the day before. We couldn't possibly go anywhere else.

Haikou port on the huge island of Hainan was our first stop. A coach arrived, with a beautiful Chinese guide, and we were off to explore the surroundings. Hainan was a strange place in 1993. On every side, towering high-rise, futuristic-style buildings were being built, but the roads were unbelievably poor. We moved at a snail's pace, bumping up and down over a multitude of potholes, but with plenty of time to look at the new ultra-modern structures. It was surreal. We were told China was in the process of developing the island as a rival to Hong Kong, which was then still under British rule.

A shocking scene, and one I can never forget, was that of a lorry moving slowly alongside us, stacked with bamboo baskets all holding individual pigs, with those on the top layer burnt red in the sun whilst the sorry animals beneath must have been suffocating in the heat. It was an horrific experience for our western eyes.

After a tranquil visit to the 'Five Officials' Memorial Temple, we were taken to a bustling indoor market. Once we had got used to the smell, we had a fascinating hour. The stall holders were charming and, of course, their wares so exotic. I stopped in my tracks at the sight of a stall displaying six reddish, glistening fish. I just had to take a photo, they were so unusual and so few of them. This eventually proved to be a wise decision.

As we all came out of the market into bright sunlight, we suddenly realised we were the subject of great attention. Half of Haikou, it seemed, had congregated to see us, and a small dais had been erected, and on top of a wooden desk there was a large, open visitors' book. The word had spread that some unusual strangers were in town. We were solemnly watched as we were invited to sign the big red book. It was a strange experience. Hainan obviously hadn't had many western visitors by 1993. The last may have been when an American Air Force plane and crew had been detained there some years ago. We bade a respectful farewell to our hosts and returned to *Caledonian Star*. Tomorrow we would be arriving in Vietnam.

After tea, as we sailed away from Hainan Island across the Gulf of Tonkin, we enjoyed a lecture by our young French guide, Phillipe, whose grandfather had been a doctor in South Vietnam. Phillipe, for all his tender years, had a wealth of knowledge of the country and its difficult relationship with the West.

The following day we arrived at Haiphong Port for Hanoi, and our first real taste of Vietnam. We waited as a large group of customs officers and various officials came on board. It was immediately apparent this was a new experience for them, and they made the most of it as, lighting up, they relaxed into armchairs, turning it into quite a social occasion.

Our passports were intently scrutinised and we were eventually allowed to disembark. Waiting on the quayside were beautiful Vietnamese girls in the lovely silk Ao Dai, their national dress, holding out flowers to welcome us. We were to get used to this charming custom at every port of call.

After an early breakfast we embarked on a 110 km journey to Hanoi, the capital of North Vietnam. Known as the rice bowl of South East Asia, Vietnam is a surprisingly green land. Spellbound, we drove through verdant, flooded paddy fields tended by girls in conical hats, and young boys riding on water buffalo. My cousin, a doctor in public health, had warned us to keep away from pigs and paddy fields – evidently the dangerous combination needed by malarial mosquitoes. I wondered how anybody could possibly do that. Wherever we looked, it was all pigs and paddy fields!

The landscape was dotted with Viet Cong war memorials reminding us we were in North Vietnam. There was so much to take in. Crossing the Red River, we made our way to Hanoi, a virtually untouched colonial city dating from 1010.

I loved Hanoi. It was surprisingly tranquil, with tree-lined boulevards and a faded air of gentility. Hairdressers and street vendors occupied shady pavement pitches with their blue and white ceramics and neatly displayed books. We visited pavilions and pagodas, and, of course, the imposing mausoleum of Ho Chi Minh, father of modern Vietnam. How quiet the streets were, just the odd bicycle passed us.

A memorable lunch was taken in a peaceful restaurant by the side of Lake Ho Tay. Huge shrimps and piquant dipping sauces were laid out before us, and large lily pad parcels, shaped like tureens, revealed boiled rice and chick peas when their leaf lids were raised. Overlooking a tree and flower-lined lake, it was a beautiful as well as a most delicious experience.

After lunch we made our way to the Temple of Literature. A landmark of traditional Vietnamese culture, it contains Stelae of Laureates dating from 1484, all set on large stone carvings of tortoises, the symbols of wisdom and learning. It was a very peaceful place.

Finally, we were taken to Hanoi's old quarter and let loose with instructions to meet up after an hour or so. But first we were given essential advice on the safe and only way to cross the road and live to tell the tale. We were grateful. With hardly a car to be seen, the roads were absolutely crammed side to side with bicycles and scooters, plus the odd rickshaw. It was an ever advancing and unstoppable tide. Mum and I nervously, with lots of 'oohs and aahs', held hands and kept going. To stop would be really dangerous, as traffic expertly judged which way to go around us. 'Just keep moving,' we were told.

We had soon come to realise how charming and pleasant the Vietnamese people are. Shopkeepers were always smiling and, without putting any pressure on us, we found it an easy delight to browse and make our purchases of exotic carvings and musical instruments. I found a delightful small cylinder, with a lid and ornate stand, about six inches high and made entirely of cinnamon bark. Its sweet perfume is still there. In the cities we could spend US dollars, but we were soon to find the only currency in rural areas was the dong. Most items were just a few dongs, and there were many hundrèds to the dollar. Feeling weary after a long but so rewarding day, we made the return journey to *Caledonian Star* and found Willie, smiling, serving our tea.

Next day came the magical, eagerly awaited visit to Ha Long Bay. We made our way through paddy fields and markets and experienced a river crossing like no other. A rather terrifying ferry ride where, on no more than a low-sided raft separating us from the murky waters, we were crammed like sardines with fellow passengers, their bikes, livestock and large bundles and our coach. Looking over the choppy reddish water, a muddy spray flew into my mouth. 'I'm done for!' I thought. Coming to no harm at all, we eventually arrived at the port of Hong Gai on the bay where a small boat awaited us with, guess who on board? A smiling Willie, plus provisions from *Caledonian Star*. Also there to greet us with flowers were two lovely local girls in traditional Ao Dai – their filmy white silk creations rippling in the gentle breeze.

We felt as if we were part of an ancient painting, sailing on that limpid sea amongst unique limestone peaks which rise, covered in vegetation, from the waters of Ha Long Bay. Hidden amongst them were grottoes and caves, home to the boat communities who live on their small and often quite primitive vessels. Some rowed over to meet us, their catch of the day drying in silvery mounds on woven roofs and alongside their washing. It was an incredible experience for us, but for the birders that day, a disappointing one as, inexplicably, there were hardly any sea birds to be found. As the sun went down, we sailed back to port where *Caledonian Star* had now moored, and with a lot of shouting and manoeuvring going on, we eventually boarded our floating home for tea.

The next day was spent at sea en route to Da Nang, and included in the on-board activities was a lecture by Tony Soper. Up to this point our birdwatchers were still waiting for the viewings they had hoped for, and expectantly attended the lecture from our resident expert. However, and I cringe to this day, poor kind Tony, honest as always, admitted, 'What I know about Vietnamese birds you could put on a postage stamp. However, we hope to have an expert joining us at Da Nang.'

Immediately, the rustle of papers could be heard as our serious, well-connected twitchers started making their notes of complaint. Back in England, birding groups were eagerly awaiting illustrated lectures from this very trip. The atmosphere was definitely frosty.

Horror of horrors, the bird expert couldn't make it, and Tony was left to keep the show on the road. He began to look nervous. We watched films on the rainforest and cave swiftlets, but would we actually see them? The day ended with 'Chef's Dinner'. A good meal always helps!

At 6am the next morning, a pilot boarded *Caledonian Star* to guide us into Da Nang harbour. From there we set off in small vehicles for a full and quite marvellous day. Crossing the scenic Hai Van Pass, appropriately known as the Pass of the Clouds and incorporating the famous Ho Chi Minh Trail, we stopped briefly to gaze at this vast green mountainous area with its picturesque fishing villages far below.

Our first destination was the ancient capital city of Hue. Reputedly, the women of Hue are renowned for their beauty, and we were not disappointed. Waiting for us was an attractive woman professor in her pink silk Ao Dai. A gentle and informative guide, she took us around the citadel district, its beautiful and tranquil complex of palaces and the temples, while smiling white-clad monks looked on. It was a monk of this order who was famously photographed immolating himself in protest against Buddhist oppression by the government during the 1960s. Who, having seen the image of flames engulfing this poor brave man, could ever forget it? Sadly, the Imperial Forbidden City was largely destroyed in the Tet Offensive in 1968, and wherever we went in Vietnam we found evidence of the war. Not least was the obvious lack of middle-aged men, who were greatly outnumbered by the young and very old. It was a rare event to see one, and a sobering discovery. The few I remember seeing wore not the traditional conical hat but a green military helmet, favoured since the 1960s.

At midday we were treated to a scrumptious 'Royal Lunch' at the Khach San Hue hotel, accompanied by traditional music on unusual and very sweet-sounding instruments. Vietnamese food was consistently proving to be light, aromatic, and truly delicious.

After lunch we eventually made our way to Emperor Tu Duc's Tomb. Tu Duc was very short and had 104 wives, but no children! He is, however, believed to be buried elsewhere, and the unfortunate 200 workers on that tomb were beheaded so grave robbers would never find it. Amidst fragrant frangipani trees we walked through an avenue of 104 small statues of very short Mandarins, and then on to the lofty Thien Mu Pagoda overlooking the Perfume River. On the ground near the pagoda, artists spread out their delicate silk painting. I couldn't resist a lovely series of three, portraying children at various stages of development. Real treasures. Mum found two carvings of boys on buffalos, one bronze and one of intricate woodwork. Such masterly work, and for so few dollars.

Our road journey back to the boat was rather frightening, especially for me sitting right at the front. Our Vietnamese driver put his foot down and, going at quite a pace, kept nodding off! As we rattled over the Hai Van Pass in the dark, I alerted Phillipe.

'Don't worry, he knows what he's doing,' he replied.

Don't worry? I kept my eyes riveted to the sleepy fellow, ready to grab the wheel at a moment's notice. What relief when we arrived safely back at *Caledonian Star* that night. Later, remembering the flat crowded ferry crossing and hair-raising return ride, I realised how trusting we tourists are in foreign parts, when out of our normal routine.

After a good and grateful sleep, we awoke to what was going to be almost the very best day in a holiday of many 'best days': a sightseeing tour of Da Nang followed by a fascinating drive to the Cham Museum, and then on to the small riverside port of Hoi An.

On the road to Da Nang there were so many photo opportunities, and I was able to take photos of country children on their way to school, and girls, with faces covered against the sun, carrying their loads on traditional long bamboo poles. These images eventually became the inspiration for several paintings. I was immediately reminded of the little old Chinese lady who we used to see shopping around Clifton Down. Wearing traditional black trousers and tunic, she had a strange bouncing gait. This must have been the consequence of years of hard work carrying a long bamboo pole with baskets balanced at each end. The Vietnamese peasant girls walked exactly the same way as they moved quickly to the rhythm of the bouncing pole.

During our sightseeing tour of leafy Da Nang city, we were startled by a cluster of explosions, and looked around anxiously before realising it was a wedding celebration with the traditional fireworks exploding. Stepping over mounds of red paper from the spent fireworks, the groom and his bride in her red headdress waved and smiled as we passed by.

In 1975, when Vietnam was divided after the fall of the Saigon government to the Communists, Da Nang had been the scene of utter chaos. What a complex and violent history this country has, and all the while, during our visit, we were met with genuine smiles and courtesy from pleasant, hardworking people.

The Cham Museum had been founded in 1915 by the Ecole Française d'Extrême-Orient. Randomly displayed were Hindu sculptures from the Cham civilisation and Kingdom dating from the 2nd to 18th centuries. Open to the elements, there were no windows or doors, and empty plinths bore testament to frequent past looting. I was horrified to see ancient sculptures and relics lying broken and discarded amongst the trees outside the museum. Here in this peaceful white temple, we learnt how the Cham civilisation in Cambodia had been virtually wiped out by Pol Pot in the 1960s, although some Cham people still remain in the Nha Trang/Da Nang area.

Reaching Hoi An, the sight before us was a revelation. We could have been transported back to the 16th century. This inland port, with its quaint buildings and traditionally clad townspeople, was such a peaceful place, with mainly handcarts and rickshaws on the narrow streets. Our guide all that day was the wonderful Mr Cong. Of all the guides, Mum and I liked him best. Gentle and knowledgeable, he was a veritable mine of fascinating information and a truly delightful companion. In one of the traditionally built wooden houses, he pointed out through a window from where I could see five different types of roofs – Viet, Chinese, Japanese, French and Portuguese – history in just one glimpse. At lunch that day, Mr Cong said in his quiet voice, 'Ah, fish sauce. Our life blood!'

I had befriended Cindy who, like me, was keen to explore the art of Vietnam. On our way to Hoi An, Tom Schornak had recommended we look out for ancient ceramics that had been dredged up from the river and sold in the town. On his last visit, he had found a Ming plate! Cindy and I were keen to find some for ourselves, as the town historically had been an important outlet for ceramics, as well as tea and silk. Riverside 'shops' in Hoi An were just open-fronted private houses, and there, to our delight, we came across beautiful old plates, small bowls and saucers. For a few dollars we made our precious selection, all then wrapped in bits of newspaper by the shopkeepers.

Mum was especially enchanted by a visit to one of the traditional houses, built on stilts to protect it from the river. The lady of the household proudly pointed to her kitchen, which only she could enter, and the family shrine, displaying photographs of her relatives. An upstairs gallery provided a refuge for the people and their belongings from flooding. Later, walking through the town, we came to a pink-washed bridge housing a Japanese pagoda, built in the 17th century to appease a water monster which was said to cause havoc in the area. I had entered another world, and felt privileged to be amongst the few to visit at that time.

On our return to Da Nang, we stopped at a small village market which surely couldn't have changed in centuries. A crowd of country women in their conical hats sat on the ground or under bamboo shelters, displaying their wares. Luckily we had been advised to bring dongs with us that day. A dollar was refused as unknown currency!

A few dongs could purchase beautifully made baskets, food covers and brooms. Wondering what we would do with our dongs, and to the evident delight of the women, we bought as much as we could sensibly take home on the plane. It was a friendly, noisy affair, as elderly toothless women waved their dongs in happy appreciation. As we left, I wondered what awful precedent we had set. It was something to think about, but I realised if it wasn't us, it would be the tourists soon to follow into this newly emerging tourist destination.

We ended the day with a visit to Marble Mountain, where we were closely escorted to the summit by children of the marble carvers who lived at its base. Carrying trays of beautifully carved, though comparatively expensive, marble objects, they had been well instructed on the 'hard sell' by their parents. These children were already budding entrepreneurs, and no one escaped their persistent efforts! It was the only place we experienced such pressure, but the view down to China Beach from the top of the mountain was worth it. A peaceful scene now, it was there that American troops first landed in 1965. These bright children, whose conversation easily switched between English and Vietnamese, were obviously the future businessmen and women of Vietnam.

Dear Mr Cong was openly unhappy. He felt we had been pressurised to buy and believed the carvings to be much too expensive, though I am pleased to have a reminder, a beautifully carved small turtle. Thinking back to the Temple of Literature in Hanoi and the stele with turtles, perhaps it would make me wise. We were sad to say goodbye to this lovely gentleman, but time and tide wait for no man, and we had to make our way back to the boat for our final destination in Vietnam – Saigon.

When we met up with our birding group we swapped stories, only to find they had had further disappointments when patrolling the beaches south of Da Nang. Just a few waders had been spotted, and by this time poor Tony was beginning to acquire a haunted look. I felt really sorry for him. He worked so hard for us and was such a kind man, still keeping tabs on 'Miss J'. This was difficult enough without the dearth of feathered friends fuelling discontent among the party.

Tom Schornak and his wife Gail were in our bus back to the boat. Knowing more of the country and where to look for authentic souvenirs, Tom had found some rough-hewn but quite charming small wooden seals, carved with Vietnamese phrases. To my amazement and delight, he presented me with one he was told said 'happiness'. Another treasure, and such a lovely souvenir.

Back in the port of Da Nang, we passed a memorial for French sailors who had all died of malaria in the previous century. I was glad of the new drug Mefloquine I had been advised to take.

On our return to the boat, we watched a video of 'Vietnam – the 10,000 day War' and decided that extensive defoliation by Agent Orange during the last Vietnamese war had spectacularly reduced the birds' habitat, or else they had all been eaten. Poor Vietnam! We could only admire the continuing cheerful industry and hospitality of its people despite such a violent and intrusive history. The film was followed by a spectacular 'potato' dinner which naturally ended with plenty of mood-enhancing vodka, cheering even the disappointed bird watchers.

Our final day on board *Caledonian Star* was spent sailing south along the Vietnamese coast towards Saigon or, as it is now known,

Ho Chi Minh City. We had plenty of time to relax and relive the wonders of this voyage. For me, it had been a truly magnificent and never-to-be-forgotten experience, a revelation – watching a deeply fascinating country on the brink of change. and witnessing parts of old Vietnam that could soon disappear.

Our birders were not quite so fulfilled. They and Tony had found quite a few in the North, but could only ponder on what might have happened to the plethora of birds they had expected. We had been supplied with a very lengthy ornithological list of species to spot during our trip. I couldn't resist writing on mine... 'Dream On!'

Sailing up the Mekong Delta towards Saigon, Tony and I got into conversation. We leaned over the boat, watching busy river traffic and waterside communities with their stilted houses and shaggy-thatched roofs. Tony's experiences in natural history and his work with the BBC made for fascinating listening. He ended our conversation with a demonstration of a honking seal, which I have to say was extremely realistic.

It was in 1976 when Saigon merged with an adjoining province, Cho Lon, and was renamed Ho Chi Minh City although it is often still also called Saigon. This was to celebrate the reunification of north and south at the end of the Vietnam War.

Leaving the boat, we said farewell to our dear, attentive Willie, Phillipe, and the Schornaks, and made our way by coach into the bustle of Saigon. What a culture shock! This was a heaving, noisy city, with none of the quiet dreaminess of Hanoi, or the green splendour and peace of the countryside. Our tour took us to temples and markets amidst really heavy traffic. We soon noticed two young men were following us on a moped with piles of t-shirts tied safely on the back. Wherever we stopped they approached us, smiling expectantly. We all politely ignored them, or said, 'No thank you', and carried on with our visits. They kept following. It was after our third stop when, from the back of the coach, I noticed how after each attempt to sell us these garments, they were most carefully folded and neatly replaced in plastic bags, then loaded on the back of the moped before the men quickly set off on our trail. I gave in, and on the next stop bought several, which turned out to be very cheap but good quality, and obviously extremely valuable to these young men.

We were due to spend our two days in Saigon at the Hotel Continental, where Graham Greene had written *The Quiet American*. However, we were to be disappointed. The hotel was overbooked and we had to stay at the nearby Hotel Cuu Long Majestic, and this was undergoing very extensive refurbishment!

I would imagine now, in the 21st Century and following its refurb, the Hotel Majestic is indeed most majestic and the height of luxury. We could definitely see evidence of future glory, but in 1993 it was a building site. Marbled halls, accompanied by the sound of running water, banging and knocking, led to our accommodation. In corridors we could actually see running water and boarded up walls, but our progress was aided at every turn by a smiling Vietnamese sentry pointing the way to safety.

Mum and I were fortunate in that our spacious room had been newly decorated and partly refurbished. A brand-new tiled bathroom, obviously unused, had been hastily cleaned, unlike the ancient, yet-to-be-replaced, heavily worn and stained carpets. I imagine these could tell quite a tale! There was some air conditioning and mosquito nets, but I wondered how many of our malarial companions would fly in through the gaps. Through dusty net curtains we looked out over a disused, flat roof area. This was home to a terribly neglected mother cat and her pathetic kittens, who knew no other life than this half existence. They were quite out of reach and never looked our way, but they are unforgettable.

Despite all, we were faring better than a single lady of our party, whose small room had no window and just wooden planks boarding up the space.

The attention and traditional food served at the Cuu Long was excellent, and the staff did everything they could to make our stay as comfortable as possible. We eventually found out they hadn't even been expecting us, and so were definitely not ready for guests. That first evening we looked into the small shop area in the hotel foyer. Mum found a traditional doll, and I spied some delicate blue and white ceramics which we promptly purchased and packed away.

The next morning we walked along adjoining Dong Khoi Street, which was filled with small family shops selling silk clothing and food. Entering one, I wondered whether I should have a pair of black silk trousers made up, and looked through the bales on display. The family assured us they could make them overnight if needed. I said I would think about it and go back if I could.

Some of our party were making a trip deep into the rural Mekong area and staying overnight in fairly primitive village ac-commodation, something I would normally love to do and with-out hesitation, but I had begun to feel unwell. It was difficult to describe, but I kept having serious palpitations and was rather weak. I hadn't been bitten, and having been told not to swallow or inhale water from the shower, I had been scrupulously obeying instructions, so I put it down to dehydration and kept swigging Coca Cola. So a quiet day was planned whilst a few of my travelling companions left without me. 'You would have so loved it, Linda,' Cindy exclaimed, with genuine sadness in her voice. Ah well!

We met up with some of our remaining party at the Continental and had a most delicious light lunch on an orchid-filled terrace. The humidity was overpowering, so we ordered coconut juice which arrived in its shell, the top chopped off for a straw. I looked over at Mum, her hair absolutely plastered to her head as she gratefully sipped away. It was so refreshing. When it came to the actual meal I wasn't quite sure what I had ordered, although I knew it was some sort of local fish. This arrived, whole and splayed out over a bed of steamed vegetables. It was a revelation in taste and presentation, and of quite superb simplicity so typical of Vietnamese food. I was still feeling a bit weak, but no worse.

Looking out over the Mekong River way down below, it was a delightful interlude, but my mind was on those silk trousers. 'I think I'll risk it,' I told Mum. We were to leave for Fraser's Hill in Malaysia at 8 am the next morning, so it could be a bit tight for time. However, on our way back to the hotel, I called into the little shop, chose some black silk, was speedily measured, and I paid up. $12.

We spent the evening packing, me still feeling unwell with palpitations as I carefully protected the precious plates from Hoi An and placed them in my hand luggage.

Down to breakfast at 7 am the next morning, expecting not to find the trousers and thinking I might have lost a few dollars, where I was presented with a neatly wrapped parcel of brown paper and string containing absolutely perfect silk trousers, and with pockets too. These have proved to be the most comfortable and useful I have ever owned. The Dong Khoi Street ladies must have worked through the night! I felt quite humbled.

As we made our way to Ho Chi Minh airport, we were briefed on procedure. Being the first group to pass through, the Customs officials would make something of it, and we must obey instructions to the letter. Four or five suitcases would be chosen for inspection and must be opened for minute inspection, while the rest of us must then, and without delay, make our way to the plane to await the others.

We arrived at the airport, wondering who would be the chosen ones, and soon became objects of great interest. Officials leaning against their counters stared solemnly at us as we passed through. Five suitcases were chosen, and the rest of us walked to the waiting Malaysian Airways plane. Suddenly, we realised we were without 'Miss J'! She had done a runner. Despite poor Tony's strenuous efforts, she was not to be found. Leaving various messages with consuls and officials, we had no choice but to leave without her.

On the plane there was a delay as we waited and waited for our companions whose suitcases had been inspected. Time went on and the plane started to rev up. Suddenly, led by a red-faced Cindy, the five burst into the plane.

'Oh, Linda. They have confiscated my plates and accused me of stealing their relics!'

After lots of red tape and form-filling, 'the guilty five' were eventually allowed to leave. Before they had even properly sat down and strapped themselves in, the plane took off. Under my seat was my hand luggage containing the precious plates. I anxiously leant forward, hands over my mouth in shock. My palpitations increased. I was a criminal, and now it was too late to do anything about it. I felt genuine guilt, but we had openly, and in all innocence, purchased the plates from a shop containing lots of them. Cindy later found one which the officials had missed at the bottom of her suitcase.

We were given water by glamorous Malaysian stewardesses, but was it safe to drink? 'We bring our own water supply,' they assured us. 'It is quite safe.' We realised we were returning to western-style civilisation, but what an incredible adventure we had had.

Arriving in Kuala Lumpur, the humidity was heavy and intense. We were grateful to sit in one of two air-conditioned coaches as our luggage was loaded. The cheerful driver had started off with a pale blue shirt, but it had turned navy blue with sweat by the time he had finished stowing the luggage. He kept smiling though. We proceeded on a long drive through dense jungle, and rubber plantations dotted with untidy townships, to Fraser's Hill, a cool retreat where we would end our holiday. This would be a guaranteed opportunity to view birdlife.

We had been travelling for quite some time when Mum said, 'Haven't we been here before?' It all looked the same to me, but perhaps this little town was familiar. She was right, our driver was lost and we had been going round in circles!

Eventually finding our way, having lost a good couple of hours, we started to climb the steepest hill I have ever known. In fact, it was a mountain, and we were on a narrow zig-zag path climbing up thousands of feet. Every so often the coach stopped, lurching backwards as the driver tried to navigate the narrow corners. Leaves of gargantuan proportions lined our way, and it was a very long drop into the jungle if our driver were to lose control for a second. We were all getting very nervous, especially as night fell and we were still on this monotonous roller-coaster. One slip and we would be headline news the next day. I could just see it – 'A coachload of UK citizens tragically left the narrow road and plunged thousands of feet into the Malaysian jungle.'

It was with the greatest relief that we eventually arrived at our hotel, but hours after Tony and the first coach. They were extremely concerned for our wellbeing, and having finished their supper should have been in bed. We had taken the wrong route up Fraser's Hill, but luckily lived to tell the tale. The other coach hadn't been without incident, one of their number becoming violently ill. On hearing that, I was glad we had been in our coach.

Frasers Hill was indeed a cool retreat, with an abundance of foliage, bird life and huge butterflies to satisfy the most exacting of naturalists. Tropical conditions forced plants to reach truly gigantic sizes, and the humble Poinsettia, bought as a small pot plant back home, grew here like a tree. Flowers were incredibly bright and beautiful; orchids cascaded as weeds from the trees. It was a truly lovely place. On a forest walk, a vivid scarlet bird flashed past me. I never found out what it was, but it was quite striking against the dark green leaves. Our hotel overlooked a golf course, which seemed rather incongruous so high up amongst the clouds, and especially in the early morning mist. However, the site was being developed with Japanese tourists in mind.

Thankfully, our return down the mountain towards Kuala Lumpur was in daylight. We gasped at the narrow winding road, with its great mist-filled precipice to one side and plants displaying leaves the size of a small roof. It looked quite surreal, almost prehistoric, and how grateful we were not to have seen this on our precarious nocturnal ascent.

We then heard that 'Miss J' was eventually located, found by British expats in a Hanoi bar, duly delivered to the Consulate and, no doubt, speedily dispatched home!

The long flight back to the UK gave us an opportunity to relive our amazing few weeks in South East Asia, although I was still feeling rather unwell. At home it became apparent to my doctor that I was suffering from a reaction to the malarial drug Mefloquine. This was to turn into weakness and a slight depression on top of the ME, which, although I managed to hide it from family and friends, lasted three years; and then, as if at the flick of a switch, it suddenly disappeared, leaving just the ME.

I wouldn't have missed Vietnam for all the world, and from then on, my career as an artist really took hold. I embarked on a series of paintings, including many versions of 'On the road to Danang' and the red fish in the Haikou market. Later I produced versions of Ha Long Bay, buffalo boys and paddy fields and beautiful girls making the conical hats. Such inspiration.

TRAVELS 1994–2000

Bonn (1994)

FOR THE NEXT FEW years I didn't feel well enough to travel too far afield. I maintained a low profile, but made the most of this quiet period with occasional excursions to Peter's class and experiments with painting at home. I continued to quietly work away in my studio with the radio for companionship, but without any real expectations of becoming a 'proper' artist. Being virtually self-taught has its pluses, but also, of course, its negatives. The negatives are constant feelings of not being accepted without a degree in art, but for me, the pluses outweigh. I was able to progress at my own speed, and not be forced into someone else's style or into the latest fad. The quiet isolation really helped, and I could pace myself without any pressures on my time. Some days I could work well, whilst others were quite testing; but I definitely progressed and, in time, became more confident.

Having kept in contact with my old friend Anne-Marie, as her career progressed from university teaching to Cultural Attaché with the French Foreign Office, invitations arrived to stay in her various postings. My brother John and his wife Lizzie visited her in what was then a heavily polluted, although fascinating, Krakow, but before I felt well enough to go myself, Anne-Marie was posted to Bonn. Another invitation arrived.

In the summer of 1994, Mum and I arrived at Anne-Marie's apartment for a week's stay in this multicultural diplomats' town. Anne-Marie, being Anne-Marie and very French, made regular trips over the border to Belgium for food shopping! We enjoyed days out in Brussels and a dampish Lisieux, where we took shelter in a small café and enjoyed stupendous whole apple dumplings just oozing with syrup to accompany our coffee. However, the prize for me was the city of Bonn and a visit to Beethoven's House, my favourite composer. How wonderful it was to actually be where the tortured genius was born, to enter the rooms he moved in and stare in awe at the piano his fingers actually touched.

Bathed in the glow of Beethoven's mastery and humming bits of his music, we moved on to modern art at the Kunst Museum. Here I came across examples of two artists I had come to admire, Franz Marc and August Macke. These two young men, German expressionists, produced joyous works of art, but were never to fulfil their potential. Both died in the Great War, Macke in France in 1914 and Marc at Verdun in 1916. I often wonder how they would have developed, and what else they would have produced for the world. However, their legacy remains, as they greatly influenced their friend Kandinsky who, with Marc, founded the famous 'Blaue Reiter' movement pioneering German Expressionism.

Another artist I admire is Modigliani, and on a day trip to Cologne, after the obligatory visit to the impressive Dom, we found Museum Ludwig and an exhibition of his drawings. I so love his confident and distinctive elongated style. A final treat together was coffee in an open-air restaurant overlooking the Rhine. Our short stay was soon over in just under a week, but it was a sunny, happy time, and a great opportunity to catch up with Anne-Marie again.

First Exhibition (1995)

This year heralded a big step forward in my development as an artist. My GP, Dr Griselda Goodden, invited me to hold the first art exhibition in their newly enlarged Pembroke Road surgery, where bright waiting room walls just begged to be filled. I jumped at the offer and made the required appointment with the practice nurse to discuss arrangements.

I was to exhibit for a whole month from 26th June to 28th July, with a donation from any sales to the Dr. Valerie Peet Memorial Fund, and I was only too pleased and grateful to comply. Dr. Peet had previously been my GP and a lovely young woman, but who tragically died during her second pregnancy. However, when I mentioned I had about twelve paintings to hang, the nurse said, 'Oh, we want lots more. Lots!'

There followed a feverish couple of months when I, 'chained' to my easel, produced paintings at a rate of knots. Animals, flowers, birds, views of Bristol, Scotland, Vietnam and Whitley Bay. I churned them out. It couldn't have been a better development experience, resulting in me becoming single-minded and more confident as a real artist.

Luckily, I had recently found an excellent local framer, the wonderfully anarchic Oscar. This dear chap framed away for all his life was worth, even up to the very morning of the exhibition, with my final painting of our pretty cat Fifi in her basket. He then gathered us up, paintings, packaging and me, and off we sped in his old car to the surgery for an afternoon's hanging. It was so very exciting.

Every so often I would pop into the surgery to find a red dot scattered here and there. One of the first paintings to sell was 'At the Fishmarket – Haikou', my representation of the fascinating red fish I had seen in the market on Hainan Island in 1993. Then my 'Seagull at Newlyn' was sold. What a great feeling it was, knowing people actually liked my work enough to buy. On the

last afternoon, with the help of Mum, John, and friends Mollie
and Sandy Brown, I set about dismantling the exhibition. This
had to be completed by evening surgery, when the room would
quickly fill up with patients. Midway through the process, as we
were busily taking pictures down, doors opened and a stream
of last-minute visitors poured in. Amongst them was dear Aun-
tie-in-law Madge in her wheelchair, being pushed along by her
son Richard. Pictures were hastily unpacked and propped up on
chairs for very last-minute viewings, and purchases were made. It
was only just in time, as patients started arriving in some numbers
and obviously needing those chairs!

What a great opportunity it was, and a huge boost to my confidence. Never again did I have to work at such a rate, but it
was a rewarding experience, and so good to know I successfully
managed it! Mollie Brown had been a great support and often
said 'Never throw anything out' when I was disappointed with a
painting. Wise words. On one occasion, after a brief unproductive
spell, she said, 'Try a little still life'. Inspired, I got to work and
painted a pig.

I was still making lace and loving it, but soon found painting
was taking over from this gentle, time-consuming pastime, which
became more of a sporadic sideline.

A voice from the past called that summer. I was invited to tea
with the Lord Mayor at the Mansion House on the Promenade,
Clifton. The Lord Mayor that year was Councillor Joan MacLaren,
who had been head physiotherapist at Bristol Maternity Hospital
during my training, and had seen me through my pregnancies.
I still remember her sitting with me, quietly going through the
breathing exercises just before my first son David was born. She
displayed such kind calmness, and her presence was a great,
much-needed support. A few months earlier, Mrs MacLaren used
me as a model in an NHS film demonstrating physiotherapy tech-
niques during pregnancy and childbirth. I was especially large
at the time, but she succeeded in finding a suitable leotard for

me to wear! This was from theatrical costumiers who had been adamant that a large enough garment would not be available. I still remember her comment, 'If you supply actors of all sizes, you can certainly find one for my little girl!' They came up with the goods.

Tea and the tour around the Mansion House with fellow guests was such a lovely experience. We felt privileged to be able to see the valuable municipal silver, furniture and paintings in this beautiful building. My old school had been just a few doors up; still called Duncan House, but by then belonging to the Midland Bank, I walked past it on my way home, recalling with a strong sense of déja-vu the activity in and out of the building, and our girlish shrieks as we played on the grassy triangle opposite.

The year progressed and I decided to paint more pictures of the Haikou fish. I was fascinated by the way they lay on the wet marble and eventually completed six works, including one in oil. Interestingly enough they all sold, and the owners were keen to know the name of the fish, which, of course, I didn't know. Amid the heat, smell and language difficulties of that busy market, I hadn't thought of asking. Another lesson learnt.

Mollie and Sandy were soon to visit Hong Kong, so I gave them my original photograph and asked if they would make some enquiries for me. I eagerly awaited their return. However, they came home without any information at all. No one recognised the fish, and no book on South East Asia gave any clue to their origin. What a mystery. A couple of years later I happened to tell the story to Mervyn, a neighbour who worked for the Rivers Authority. He believed he could help. Off he went with the photograph to contact colleagues at the International Marine Laboratory in Plymouth. Time went by, and I forgot all about it until, looking out of my window one day, I saw Mervyn walking quickly towards the house with a smile on his face and holding a sheaf of papers. An exciting discovery had been made. Scientists at the laboratory had embarked on enthusiastic research and decided the famous fish were South American Red Bellied Piranhas! The evidence was supported by several documents with photos and extensive highlighting in red.

The letter from the Director, Professor R Fauzi C Mantoura, reads

'Dear Mervyn,

IDENTIFICATION OF PHOTOGRAPHED FISH FROM HAINAN ISLAND OFF VIETNAM

I have sought views from fish biologists at the PML with fascinating if not intriguing response – you seem to have got some South American piranhas on the fishmonger's slab off Vietnam!

I attach Nick Halliday's briefing note together with a copy of George Myer's monograph on piranha, in which he suggests we are dealing with serrasalmus nattereri.

I am taking a second opinion on this intriguing identification since, although piranhas are fished and eaten in South America, their export (if that is what has happened) is forbidden.

I trust this helps.

Best wishes,

Yours sincerely,

R Fauzi C Mantoura

No wonder there were only six fish! Some poor Chinese farmer had obviously been nurturing his meagre stock from wherever he had managed to procure the originals, and was only able to produce a few at a time! I hoped this wasn't going to cause trouble, but Mervyn assured me that, rather than any desire to follow it up, the find had simply generated genuine excitement that specimens had reached China and were being sold at a market. Such a relief.

Sue Edney, a friend and fellow artist from Peter Clay's group, suggested I should submit a painting to Clifton Arts Club Annual Open Exhibition. Sue came from a family of established Slade trained artists, and she was certainly very professional in her work, so I felt encouraged and decided to take the plunge. On 'sending-in' day I took along my pig picture, titled 'Love You', and kept my fingers crossed. I would find out whether it had been selected at the Private View. A few weeks later, feeling very nervous, I arrived at the Private View evening and anxiously scanned the catalogue. Lo and behold, my name was there; 'Love You' had indeed been selected. What a thrill. It was the very beginning of my ongoing relationship with this illustrious art club.

Founded in 1906 by four Academicians, most of the club's early members were professional artists. Jacques-Emile Blanche, the first President, had been a student of Manet, and early exhibits included loan pictures by Monet, Whistler, Matisse and Stanley Spencer. With its impressive history, Clifton Arts Club had a waiting list of several years, but Sue persuaded me to put my name forward and she would propose me. Pat Corrigan, the membership secretary, seconded me, and I joined a long, expectant queue.

Paris (1996)

March arrived and Anne-Marie was to receive her doctorate in mediaeval theatre at the Sorbonne. After a difficult marriage and a very traumatic seven-year legal process, she had at last managed to divorce her husband and wanted us to be there in support as her 'family', so Mum and I went to Paris.

The Petit Palais had a major Corot Exhibition, and I had so hoped Anne-Marie could get tickets for us. 'Impossible,' she announced. They were like gold dust and she was unsuccessful, but I was still pretty determined to get there. How could I come to Paris and not at least make the effort?

The doctorate ceremony would be held over three days, from the Friday afternoon to Sunday, and so, on the first day, we arrived at the Sorbonne and found a small auditorium where the proceedings were to be held. The room slowly filled up. We were in for a gruelling few days.

Anne-Marie came into the auditorium and sat at a single desk, preparing her papers. She looked smart and chic as only the

French can, her hair absolutely immaculate. Then, five Professeurs entered and took their places, facing Anne-Marie on the dais. Each had a very large, beautifully bound copy of Anne-Marie's thesis placed before them. They proceeded to question her. It seemed as if we were witnessing an interrogation Originally I had thought there would be some sort of short ceremony, Anne-Marie would be awarded her doctorate, then we would celebrate with champagne and cakes. In reality it was so different. We all knew she was to be awarded the doctorate, but first she had to undergo this continual and intense questioning for several hours. The room was getting hotter and hotter.

Poor Anne-Marie, normally so assured and confident, was actually nervous, and her words came out in a strangled fashion. Goodness, could those Professeurs talk, and at such great length! This event must have cost Anne-Marie a fortune - not just the expensive suit and hairdo, but with the six beautifully bound theses plus post-ceremony refreshments. By this stage I was desperate for refreshment.

That evening, Anne-Marie said, 'Why don't you have tomorrow off and come back to the Sorbonne later in the afternoon?' It was music to my ears. We had Sunday to catch up with the doctorate, and there was plenty of Paris to see first.

'We could go to the Corot,' I suggested.

'You could try, but you won't get in,' Anne-Marie replied.

The following morning we set off, eventually reaching the Petit Palais by 11 o'clock to join a very long queue. Twenty minutes later a man appeared and cut the queue off directly behind us. His arm came down and all those waiting after us were told they would not get in. We had managed it! Up the steps and in we went.

The self-taught and prolific Corot produced delightfully atmospheric landscapes, street scenes and portraits which seemed to melt and glitter. It was a glorious exhibition. For me, best of all were his views from the Palatine over ancient Rome. I made an instant decision. The artist in me was taking over. I had to stand where he did and experience Rome for myself.

We spent a couple of hours at the Corot before an obligatory visit to the riches of the Musée d'Orsay. Then, pleasantly saturated with art, we returned to the Sorbonne for the last hour of that day's rigorous proceedings.

Thankfully, the following morning, Anne-Marie was awarded her exceptionally well-deserved doctorate and we all retired for refreshments and some relaxed banter with our fellow guests and Les Professeurs. Les Professeurs were actually quite light-hearted and amusing outside the interrogation room.

Later that day, together with a few other friends, we were treated to a particularly relaxed and delicious bistro supper. I remember the meal to this day, and have often tried, sometimes successfully, to reproduce it: grilled Crottin de Chavignol (the solid disc-shaped goats' cheese), on a bed of red salad leaves with toasted walnuts and walnut dressing. Absolute heaven!

It was such a privilege to be with my old friend and to share this important occasion with her. On Monday we said our goodbyes and promised to visit again.

As we left Paris, we were immediately planning our next trip... to the Eternal City: Rome. Rob was still in his Christian pop group, 'Kapitaan', with his friend Anthony Gorry. The Gorrys were living in Rome, attached to Interpol from the Metropolitan Police Force. They had already invited us to stay, so we contacted Anthony's parents, Joe and Christine, who suggested a visit in May. We were to stay in their home, a villa in the very grounds of the British Embassy residence.

Rome (1996)

A spectacular thunderstorm heralded our arrival in Rome. Rob and Anthony had obviously described us very accurately as we were immediately recognised in Arrivals. Christine called out, 'Hellooo. I knew it was you!' We hugged and set off.

We could hardly believe our eyes as we arrived in the Lateran district. The sun came out as we swept through ornate Embassy gates. Guards waved in acknowledgment as we proceeded up the wooded drive to the villa. It was beautiful.

Adjoining part of the old city wall, the Gorrys' charming villa was light, airy and cool, despite the increasing temperature of the day. Immediately made to feel so welcome, we knew we were in for a special week.

The following morning we walked through the main gates, pausing a while to talk to the gatekeeper, Ferdinando, and his huge black guard dog, Bruno, before exploring the area. It was so central. Nearby was the impressive statue of St Francis of Assisi, his arms open wide, facing the cathedral church of San Giovanni in Laterano. We entered its cool interior and admired the lovely old cloisters, which later became a suitable subject for one of my pastel paintings.

Taking a steep side road in the opposite direction, we passed a small church from where the most beautiful singing soared. Outside, the narrow road was in the process of being re-cobbled, and a young builder paused for me to take photographs of him with his traditional cobbling tools. These looked as if they hadn't changed for centuries. Further down the hill we came across a busy local fruit and vegetable market. Jewel-like displays of local produce were shaded from the hot sun, with local people making their purchases. It was a bustling, happy place, and then, suddenly, we arrived at the Colosseum. Here before us was one of the most famous and recognisable monuments in the world.

As we walked through this imposing relic, I could almost hear the roar of Roman citizens appreciating the powerful spectacles played out before them. A little further we came across partly derelict underground chambers, which must have accommodated animals and prisoners as well as gladiators. This area was covered in poppies, and we felt a powerful sense of brooding. It was a sad place.

Rome is known as the city of cats, and it is indeed a very feline-friendly place. Cats of every colour amble easily around or lie contentedly in the sun. Petted and regularly fed, they appear calm and confident and, in many cases, rather superior!

We moved on to the Forum. I was bowled over by the incredible beauty and majesty of the place. It was as if we were standing as extras in a film set. Time was going on, and we hurried to the Palatine, but to my great disappointment I was unable to stand exactly where Corot did; there was a fence there. Still, I was near enough, and able to absorb its true splendour as evening light bathed us in a golden glow. We made two visits to the Vatican, a vast city itself within the city of Rome. The first was most fortunately made on a weekday, and we found it especially quiet and pleasant, giving us plenty of time and space to enjoy the multitude of treasures within. I think my favourite exhibit was the Map Room – one of the many highly decorated corridor rooms – although at every turn there were exquisite statues, paintings, tapestries and chapels, and, of course, the recently renovated Sistine Chapel. We looked up in awe at the famous ceiling, displaying the genius of Michelangelo, gazing at the lofty extravaganza above us until our necks ached. A week could be spent in the Vatican alone, but we had to make do with two days. Returning the following Saturday, the crowds were huge, which made progress and viewing very uncomfortable. How fortunate we were to have caught that quiet moment earlier in the week. During the first visit we came across a huge marble of a horse and chariot. 'Pretend you are about to climb in,' I told Mum. 'It will make a great photo.' 'Certainly not,' she said. Another opportunity missed.

One evening we walked with the family by the River Tiber in Trastevere and were treated to a 'proper' pizza supper by Joe, Christine, and their daughter Joanne. We had found this sweet young girl to be such good company for one so young. In the warm evening we enjoyed happy banter as we tucked into our very tasty traditional pizzas. Under a Bristol Blue night sky, we finished the evening off with a walk through quaint streets to the glorious Piazza Navona and Pantheon. I remember Robert saying how you couldn't turn a corner in Rome without seeing some majestic monument.

We wanted to take the family out for Sunday lunch, and left it to them to choose their favourite place. When Sunday arrived, off we all went to the Caracalla Baths where, tucked right behind, was the most delightful family restaurant. We would never have found it on our own. On a shady netted terrace, full of flowers and surrounded by Roman families, we tucked into delicacies such as stuffed courgette flowers and perfectly grilled swordfish, followed by home-made ice cream. It was gorgeous!

'You must taste something,' said Joe. He ordered Limoncello and we had our first experience of this delightful liqueur. I am now never without it, always kept in the freezer to maintain its frosty deliciousness.

Christine had arranged for the three of us to visit the Pope's private garden at Castel Gandolfo, just outside Rome. This was a rare treat, with only 500 visitors a year allowed, but made possible for us by another ex-pat who was attached to the Holy See. A rainy morning dawned and, undaunted, off we drove to Castel Gandolfo. Joining a small group, we sheltered under our umbrellas as we waited outside the main gates for security clearance. Miraculously, the rain stopped as we entered. We were not allowed to take anything with us as we walked around the garden, so no photographs on this occasion, but the beauty and tranquility of the place remains imprinted on my memory. Perched imposingly high above a lake, the garden reminded me of Versailles, but with Roman artefacts. I could visualise the then Pope, John Paul II, wandering and meditating in this private, much-loved beauty spot.

After our morning in the Pope's garden, we drove around the lake to the Convent of Palazzola. Owned by the English College in Rome, it is a retreat and guest house for travellers. In charge was Father Grimshaw, aided by his smiling assistants, Sisters of Mercy Madeleine, Gertrude and Baptiste.

Taken to a refectory, we tucked in to great quantities of pasta, thinking this was the main meal, but it was then followed by a substantial chicken casserole! We drank wine from tumblers which we then kept for our coffee. It was simple, delicious, abundant food served by the gentle nuns. Then genial Father Grimshaw opened his drinks cabinet to display a truly vast array of bottles. Whatever you wanted would be found there.

We were escorted around the historic Palazzola by an English trainee priest. He was an excellent guide, and we learned the amazing history of the 'little palace'. Dating from 125 BC when the Scipio family occupied the property, it became the home of Benedictines in 1025, then the Augustinians in 1210, followed by Franciscan Friars from 1460 to 1910. In 1910 the Portuguese Friars left during their Civil War, and the palace became a Colonia di Salute for overweight people. Purchased by the English School in 1920, it was briefly occupied by German medical officers in 1944 when the English college returned to England. In 1946 anti-war frescoes were found painted on the refectory walls. In the chapel we even found a stone plaque in Latin, which mentioned a connection to Clifton cathedral!

'Geo. Ambrosius. EP. Cliftonien'

Soon we would have to bid our farewells to the Gorry family, but we just had a few more essential visits to fit in first. There was so much to see, and we only had a week. The romantic Trevi Fountain and Spanish Steps beckoned, then a quick foray into the Villa Borghese, followed by the Basilica of Santa Maria Maggiore, before a last look at San Giovanni in Laterano.

It was here, armed with my camera, I was approached by a young, very plump and rather poorly-dressed priest. He couldn't speak English, but made it known he would like me to take his photo in front of San Giovanni. It was a busy day with people milling around, but he obviously picked us out as trustworthy. He gave his bags to Mum and handed me his cracked camera that was taped up with sticking plaster. Theatrically, he arranged his pose. I say pose, for what an uncanny performance it was. He must have practised this at home in front of his mirror. Standing proudly with one foot on a low wall, he folded his arms high on his swelling chest, and with a generous square-cut chin thrust forward, he signalled he was ready. I could have been photographing a young Mussolini! I imagined this precious photo was to be taken back to his country parishioners, who would look on it with awe and respect.

I left Rome, this wonderfully warm and romantic city, overflowing with marvellous memories. Surely you haven't lived until you have seen Rome!

DEVELOPING AS AN ARTIST AND EXHIBITING

O N OUR RETURN MY painting started in earnest, and towards the end of the year I was actually beginning to feel a little better. During my trips to Paris, Bonn, and Rome, I certainly felt slightly below par, but it certainly didn't spoil anything for me. The strangest thing: almost exactly three years to the very day I had originally succumbed to the depression and weakness after Vietnam, it just went away as if a switch flicked, and the cloud was gone. I still suffered from crippling migraines and exhaustion if I overdid it, but at least I was back to my normal happy self. Mefloquine, or Larium as it is known, probably prolonged the chronic fatigue, but this depression never happened again. Needless to say, I would now be prescribed different anti-malarial pills if needed.

My artistic progress had some exciting developments that year. First, a poster in a local shop advertised 'Art in the Shrubbery'. I decided I must visit, as it was only a short walk away in the adjoining suburb of Redland.

This beautiful, well-presented exhibition of paintings and ceramics, held in the home of Sue and David Lodge, was an annual event. I actually went twice, taking Robert with me the second time, and he was just as enthusiastic. We both made small purchases. I introduced myself to Sue, who, with David, eventually visited me at home. I was thrilled to find they liked my work and invited me to exhibit at the next 'Art in the Shrubbery'. It was a huge step forward. Surely I was now a 'proper' artist.

By then I had also been invited to hang some pictures in a new café at the end of the road. The owners were John and Pam Mitten, and John's father was the great Charlie Mitten of soccer fame! Known as 'The Bogotá Bandit' in the 1950s, Charlie Mitten had been one of the first footballers to play for a foreign team. I was so excited; this was footballing royalty, and I hoped I might be able to meet him and shake his hand one day. I was longing to share all this, but the only other person who would appreciate it and be as thrilled as me was Dad, unfortunately long gone. I felt quite sad, but consoled myself with a good session with my old footballing books.

In the autumn of that year in 'Harold Hockey', our famous local art supply shop, I met up with fellow pastel artist Sarah Summers. 'Look at this!' She called me over and proceeded to show me a colourful leaflet. 'A charity has included some of my designs in their Christmas card selection.' I opened the leaflet and admired her beautiful festive elephants. 'They'll definitely sell,' I replied. 'I'd buy them. In fact, I could sell them at my Christmas coffee morning.' For a couple of years I had organised a small Christmas bazaar at home. More of a get-together for neighbours, it included a Tearcraft Christian Fair Trade stall, a Bring and Buy, and was becoming a popular local event.

As I read on through the leaflet, I was very taken with the actual charity. Founded by a young David Constantine, after a diving accident in Australia resulting in quadriplegia, the organisation produced wheelchairs for Third World countries. Three things about it caught my interest: 1) The wheelchair element (being a physio); 2) Its headquarters and workshops based in Brockley where I had lived; and 3) Sarah's charming designs. I decided to contact them straight away. It was my first experience of 'Motivation', and the beginning of a long and fruitful artistic relationship.

1997 proved to be a good year for more progression. That May, Sue and David Lodge held their 'Art in the Shrubbery' weekend as usual, and I was invited to take part and join fellow artists in what was to be a very successful and well-organised exhibition. I sold several paintings, including one of tulips to Mischa Scorer who had recently produced a programme about Degas for the BBC. I was absolutely thrilled. He had wanted 'The Cloisters, San Giovanni in Laterano', but James had arrived earlier and insisted this one was for him. The red dot was already on by the time Mischa arrived!

Another boost came in the summer with the Clifton Arts Club Open Exhibition, and I exhibited my third picture of the notorious fish in Haikou. It is a wonderful feeling, having the approbation of your peers. I hoped it would last.

In October, as part of the Cabot 500 and Bristol International Friendship Year, Bristol solicitors Burroughs Day held an exhibition called 'Artists Celebrate Bristol' and I was invited to participate. I had just started to work on Bristol scenes, especially the famous Suspension Bridge, including hot air balloons, for the first time. Bristol has become a major centre for hot air ballooning and an international festival is held each August.

Still having to rest frequently, I often put my feet up and looked out over the Bristol skyline towards Cabot Tower and the Dundry Hills. The skies from Worrall Road appear quite monumental, with a vast panoramic landscape and hot air balloons regularly floating by. How fortunate to be able to enjoy such a fabulous spectacle on a daily basis. I started to notice how my surroundings changed from month to month, and felt an irresistible urge to record them. 'There is no point thinking about it,' I told myself. 'Get on and do it!'

I watched as conditions of light remained the same for about four days only, and wondered whether I was up to the challenge of recording a whole year. It would be quite a commitment, but I was determined to give it a good go. 1998 arrived, and in the February I made a start on what was going to be a rather anti-social twelve months. Pastel, being a very permanent medium, stains easily, and is difficult if not impossible to remove, so my sitting room carpet had to be covered in newspaper for protection. Coloured dust and trodden-in bits of pastel still turn up in the most unexpected places though. So, with my easel angled in front of the large picture window, several boxes of pastels and accessories at hand, I faced the challenge.

With the best light occurring first thing in the morning and last thing in the afternoon, I had to be extremely disciplined, Often I found myself in pyjamas hours later, and, beginning to feel rather peckish after such an early start, I hoped no one would call. When painting was underway it was very difficult to stop, but by about nine o'clock the light had changed so I had to leave it until the next morning, or start a new work later when warm evening light bathed my increasingly interesting view. I stuck to the task, becoming rather obsessive, but it paid off and I eventually managed to complete two or three suitable paintings each month. These were an obvious and genuine record of the Clifton Year from my view, and when August arrived so did my acceptance as a member of Clifton Arts Club. The next step would be a solo exhibition.

1998 was memorable also as the year my first granddaughter, pretty Chloe, arrived. It would be four more years before Rob and Bernice produced her brother Charlie, but after that grandchildren seemed to come along on quite a regular basis.

1999 AND THE MILLENNIUM

IN THE SPRING, ANNE-MARIE invited me back to Paris. Her son Nicolas had helped to organise a major exhibition, 'Maroc', at the Petit Palais, and we were to visit. For me, the most outstanding exhibits were the very ones Nicolas had been involved with. Huge, beautiful, pastel portraits of various ethnic groups in Morocco were prominently displayed. These were the works of the late Zinaida Serebriakova, who, originally from an aristocratic Russian family, had arrived in Paris with her children during the Revolution. Nicolas was able to meet Zinaida's elderly daughter and model, who had spent her whole life promoting her mother's work and that of her late brother, Nikolay; sadly, though, to the detriment of her own obvious talent.

Anne-Marie and I were invited to tea with Madame Serebriakova. This little bird-like lady darted from one part of her apartment to the other to show us the work of her gifted family. Zinaida's pictures were stacked high in every possible space, and her daughter heaved them out, insisting we should see and admire them all. And then there were her uncle's masterly bronzes, and, not least, many catalogues of her brother's work. A famous painter of interiors, her brother Nikolay had indeed been worthy of international acclaim. It was a joy to look through the books and admire the intricacy.

'Madame Serebriakova might show you her own work if she likes you,' Anne-Marie whispered.

I just had to ask her and she did show me, although with a fairly dismissive wave of her delicate hand. Her work was lovely, and indeed a match for the rest of the family. I felt rather sad for her as I looked through a Christie's catalogue of Nikolay's interiors, when I noticed her name, in very small print, right at the back of the album. Here she was briefly acknowledged as the painter of the most intricate parts of the paintings, such as the tiny, perfect pictures actually within their frames. Her work was so accomplished, but sacrificed for her family.

Tea was served in old Russian china, and we spent the rest of our time talking about the 'Maroc' exhibition, and hearing how the Serebriakov family estates were now being restored as an important part of Russian history. Madame asked me to send her some examples of my portraits when I returned home, which I did, of course, and with most grateful thanks for that unexpected and perfect afternoon.

The rest of my stay in Paris was taken up by compulsory visits to the Louvre, Musée d'Orsay and the Picasso Museum, with lunches in trendy Marais and tea in smart cafés alongside the Seine. Fully inspired, I spent my last afternoon in Sennelier's art shop, where I stocked up with pastels from the masters, the very firm who supplied Degas. Shelves and trays were filled with every hue of pastel and paint. It was an artist's wonderland.

The Alvis wedding season began this year. James, now playing rugby for Exeter and teaching at Blundell's School in Tiverton, met the lovely Mary: a farmer's daughter, fellow teacher and rugby player for Exeter Ladies. An engagement soon followed.

John's sister Rachael and her husband Chris loved the boys David, James and Rob, and are a doting aunt and uncle. When they found a red Alvis Coupe they bought it, together with an ALV number plate for the boys to use at their weddings. Quite remarkable, and how loving and generous.

James and Mary's wedding took place in Blundell's School chapel on a sunny July day. It was a gloriously happy occasion, although James, thinking about Grandpa, cried, of course. One down, two to go. Little did I know then that there would be Alvis weddings for three years running. Three different outfits and hats would be absolutely necessary!

1999 was the first time the charity 'Motivation' chose my pastel painting 'Robin' for inclusion in their Christmas card selection, and it was to be successfully repeated another year. The cards were printed free of charge by Ford Land Motor Company. This magical little image surprised even me by taking only twenty minutes to produce, and seeming to just appear on the pastel card. David insisted on buying it for his new fiancé, the adorable Katie, and when Ford Land saw it, they asked if they could use it themselves. I always try to remember 'less is more', and it certainly was with little 'Robin'. It is so easy to overwork an image, and I still do.

This year would end on another high note when Sue and David Lodge offered to host my exhibition 'The Clifton Year', twelve months of paintings from my view over Bristol. We planned it for October, and our local estate agents, Richard Harding, agreed to sponsor me. It was so exciting and, as it turned out, very successful. One family, undecided whether to buy September, October, or November, bought all three! Heady days.

And now the Millennium was upon us. What would this new century bring?

ALSO BY LINDA ALVIS

MEMOIR
Hoovering Up the Holy Carpet, Volume 2: New Century Travels

CHILDREN'S BOOKS
Worrall and Robin
Worrall, Robin and the Garden Visitor

POETRY
Dawn Rising

Cover Images

FRONT COVER
Dawn Rising, Clifton, Bristol
On the road to Danang, Vietnam
The Surprise, Sabi Sabi, South Africa

BACK COVER
Haikou Fishmarket, Hainan Island, China
Clifton College, Bristol
On Guard! Little Karoo, South Africa
On the Nile
Seagull, Newlyn
Ha Long Bay, Vietnam
Eiffel Tower, Paris
Duncan House School, Bristol
The Cloisters, San Giovanni in Laterano, Rome
Dream Morning, Clifton Suspension Bridge
The Boatman, Castlebay, Outer Hebrides

Photographs relating to this book can be found on my web-site at www.alvisfineart.co.uk/books. My paintings and further award-winning poems, inspired by these travels, can be found in the poetry book *Dawn Rising*.

ACKNOWLEDGEMENTS

Without the wonderful author and founder of Hawkesbury Upton Literature Festival, Debbie Young, my story would not have come to light. She has my undying gratitude. My thanks to Peter Moore who so patiently read through the manuscript and offered gentle and most valuable pointers. I will never look at a hyphen in the same way again! Thank you to Dan Gooding for his editing skills and to Jac Solomons for producing the cover so beautifully. Finally, to my friend Jenny Walmsley and my partner Mike Rome a huge thank you for continued advice, support and patience.

Printed in Great Britain
by Amazon

10905455R00084